Follow The Canning Diva®

www.canningdiva.com

T0315319

Canning Full Circle

From Garden to Jar to Table
Revised & Expanded Edition

Diane Devereaux

canningdiva.com

Patoka Press

Indianapolis, Indiana

Canning Full Circle: From Garden to Jar to Table, Revised & Expanded Edition
Copyright © 2017, 2023 Diane Devereaux, The Canning Diva®

Originally published in 2017 by Devereaux Cyber Inc.

New edition published in 2023 by Patoka Press, an Adriane Doherty Company, LLC.
Indianapolis, Indiana

Distributed by Cardinal Publishers Group, a Tom Doherty Company, Inc.
Indianapolis, Indiana
www.cardinalpub.com

All rights reserved under International and Pan-American Copyright Conventions.

No part of this book, in whole or part, may be reproduced, stored in a database, or other retrieval system, or transmitted in any form, by any means, including mechanical, photocopy, recording, or otherwise, without prior written permission of the publisher.

Disclaimer:
The Publisher and the author make no warranties or representations with respect to the completeness or accuracy of the contents of this work. All information, recipes, and advice are used at the risk of the consumer. The Publisher and author specifically disclaim all warranties, including without limitation warranties of fitness for a particular purpose. No warranty may be extended or created by sales or marketing materials. The strategies and advice contained herein may not be suitable for every situation. The Publisher and author are not responsible for any hazards, loss, or damage that may occur as a result of content's use. This work is sold with the understanding that the publisher is not engaged in rendering legal, medical, or other professional advice or services. If professional assistance is required, the services of a competent professional should be sought. The fact that an individual, organization, or website is referred to in this work as a citation and/or potential source of further information does not mean that the Publisher or author endorses the organization, website, or information that they/it may provide or recommendations they/it may make or infer. Further, readers should be aware that websites listed in this work may have changed or disappeared between when this work was written and when it is read.

ISBN 978-0-99632-470-0

Cover and Interior Photography: Jeff Hage, Green Frog Photo
Book Design: Glen Edelstein
Editor: Tessa Schmitt

10 9 8 7 6 5 4 3 2 1   23 24 25 26 27 28 29 30 31 32

Inquires about Canning Processes or Recipes should be directed to The Canning Diva® at www.canningdiva.com

Dedication

To my amazing Mumma, Linda Newton. Her unfailing love and unwavering faith in Christ is an example to us all.

Introduction

Over the past decade I have been very blessed to share the art and craft of home canning. As The Canning Diva® it has been my pleasure educating people all over the world, teaching the time-honored tradition of preserving food in glass jars. "Food sustainability" and "preparedness" are no longer buzz words but concepts many of us have put into action in recent years.

Canning Full Circle is truly an expansion of my first mission as an author – to give a full circle view of home canning and food preservation starting from the garden, into the kitchen, then onto your family table. I aspire to teach everyone the amazing benefits of this process as I show how to preserve your bounty in a jar and creative ways to use home canned goods in meals, desserts, appetizers, and even cocktails.

While I teach a great deal of pertinent information, I also give advice. Many of you know the story of my, then, toddler son who was mortified when I made his favorite applesauce blue using blueberries. My over-zealous excitement to create this fun treat for my son prompted me to can 22 pints of a recipe my son will never eat; hence my need to make blueberry applesauce muffins. It was from this lesson the original book idea was born as was the advice I still give to this day, *"If you won't eat it, don't can it!"*

Over the years, my advice is still flowing but the message has changed given today's landscape.

"Preparedness over fear" has become my mantra in a world riddled with unknowns and major changes. Sadly, some changes not for the better. As food preservationists, we have peace of mind knowing what we 'put-up' in our pantry for our families will sustain us in hard times.

Controlling what we can starts in our kitchens as home canners. We know what ingredients go into every jar, giving us the assurance that we are doing right by our bodies. We work diligently to grow and raise what we are able to, so we may offset the logistical and supply chain shortcomings in the commercial food arena. And, we have gotten quite crafty at locating good deals and finding new sources for food and canning supplies. But best of all, we have created a beautiful international community of like-minded individuals banding together to support our fellow canners.

I am so excited to share the revised and expanded *Canning Full Circle*. We have worked diligently to give this book a face lift, making it cleaner and easier to read. I have created new canning recipes and uses for your home canned goods, expanding your minds and your palates. And my amazing friend and food photographer, Jeff Hage, has done an outstanding job (AGAIN) capturing the essence of every recipe and bringing the food to life.

So, grab your canning supplies and let's head into the kitchen. We have some canning to do!

xo
Diane, The Canning Diva®

Table of Contents

Table of Contents

• To The Jar Recipe
▪ **To The Table Recipe**

CHAPTER 1

Food Preservation Basics

Filled with answers to your many home canning questions, this chapter will provide an overview of home canning basics so you feel confident water bathing and pressure canning food. Learn the basics of how to safely can, the science of how we are able to preserve food long-term, and various tips and techniques for a successful canning season.

A Little History

Many of you may not know this, but canning dates back to the Napoleon War era starting in 1803. In a nutshell, Napoleon was losing the war on the front line, because his men were without food – and without food, his men couldn't sustain. "An army marches on its stomach," Napoleon famously said. By the time fresh foods would make it to the front, it would be rotten and inedible, leaving his men to pillage or purchase whatever the native country had to offer.

Napoleon put it to his people: whomever could find a way to preserve large quantities of foods to sustain their soldiers would receive a 12,000 franc reward. Nicholas Appert collected the prize, already knowing that food cooked within a glass jar would not spoil unless exposed to oxygen, hence the need for a good sealing lid. He developed this method of jar sealing not realizing just how necessary it would become.

Fast forward about 50 years and Louis Pasteur discovered how time, temperature, and acidic value play a vital role is protecting us from harmful microbes by outlining how to properly process foods. In November 1946, a team of four individuals worked diligently to publish a standardized method of safe canning practices for low acid foods in the United States. This group included Edward Toepfer, a technologist; Howard Reynolds, a bacteriologist; Gladys Gilpin, a food specialist; and Katherine Taube, a household equipment specialist. Their work laid the foundation for pressure canning food in the home.

Later, their white paper titled, "Home Canning Processes for Low-Acid Foods," developed the basis of heat penetration and inoculated packs and was adopted by the United States Department of Agriculture (USDA) in January 1947.

Today, our expansion in technology and food science continues to develop vital methods for managing a sustainable food source – especially in everyday homes.

Three Key Pillars of Home Canning

Throughout my many years of teaching canning classes, I begin every class with the basics. Whether you are a veteran canner or a beginner, I make it my job to teach everyone the reasons why we are able to do what we do in our home kitchens. At the forefront are Time, Temperature, and Acidic Value.

Let's break it down...

Acidic Value

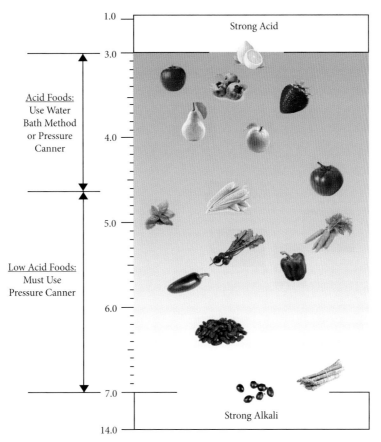

The pH value of foods varies based on many factors. Always follow trusted canning recipes for safety.

Food naturally has a pH value. Sometimes that value registers little to no acid; other times it can be highly acidic. On the pH scale, numbers demonstrate the acidic value meaning the higher the number on the scale, the lower the acidic value and vice versa.

When it comes to the acidic value of food, please do not confuse pH acidic value with *flavor*. Let me ask you, what do you think has more acidity, a sweet strawberry or a hot habanero pepper? The answer: a sweet strawberry (3.5 pH) has a higher acidic pH value than a hot habanero pepper (5.8 pH). Spicy or hot *tasting* foods do not mean a higher acidic value on the pH scale.

Why Acidity is Important

The reason we must understand a food's acidic value is without the presence of acid when canning, harmful bacteria will grow. Some bacteria will continue to grow in an **anaerobic environment**. **Botulism**, a well-known bacterium, can only grow in an anaerobic environment. Some foods that grow underneath the ground, such as potatoes, naturally have botulism bacteria on their skin because they grow in an oxygen-free environment.

Home canning doesn't produce botulism; rather, the bacteria spore must be present in the first place for it to inhabit the food. Since botulism naturally exists throughout the earth, air, and soil, canners learn how to prevent botulism from inhabiting their food by using proper food cleaning and preparation methods. Furthermore, canners comprehend how the three key pillars of home canning work to keep food stored in jars safe.

Another major factor with respect to acidic pH value is to consider the sum of all foods in one recipe, not just the main ingredient. Take, for instance, salsa. Although the main ingredient is tomatoes, which have a mid-grade level of pH acidity, it is the sum of all ingredients combined that count when home canning. Once you start adding onions, jalapeños, cilantro, corn, and black beans, you now have diluted, or neutralized, the salsa's overall acidic value.

So, what do you do when a recipe is lacking acidity? One option is to add acid.

Acid can be in the form of lemon juice, lime juice, vinegar, or wine. When shopping for these products, the key is to ensure the label clearly states a minimum of 5% acidity. If it is not 5% acidity or higher, do not use it for home canning to elevate the acid, especially when pickling. Save diluted vinegars for fresh recipes, vinaigrettes, or cleaning.

Another option is to increase the processing time which we will dive into next.

Time & Temperature

Time and temperature refer to the second stage of canning, which is called **processing**. The recipe's overall acidic value and density dictate the proper processing method and time.

There are two processing methods: water bathing and pressure canning. Each method is defined by its temperature output. Water bathing temperature output is 212°F, because we rely on the temperature of boiling water to safely process our jars of food. Pressure canning however, gives a temperature output upwards of 250°F so we may safely process low acid foods more efficiently. The length of time a jar of food processes is dictated by the food's overall acidic value and the temperature required to kill harmful foodborne pathogens.

High Acid Foods

In my water bath recipes throughout *Canning Full Circle*, you will note I share not to start the timer until the water is at a **full rolling boil**. A full rolling boil is the only way to visually ensure the water temperature is at 212°F, which is the required temperature to kill harmful pathogens in acidic foods. A recipe with an overall high acid content of 4.6 pH or less can be safely water bathed because the temperature, in combination with the bacteria killing acid, are sufficient for long-term storage.

Low Acid Foods

Foods such as root crops and meat do not have a high acid content. These foods range from 4.6 pH or higher on the pH scale, meaning they are naturally low in acid, so we must either add acid or rely on time and temperature to safely kill harmful bacteria during processing. And I don't know about you, but I certainly do not want to pickle my chicken to keep it safe. So, the only way to process low acid foods is to expose it to a high enough temperature long enough to do the trick.

Bacteria, yeast, and mold grow fastest between temperatures of 40°F and 140°F. When canning low acid foods, the temperature required to kill harmful bacteria, yeast, and mold without the presence of acid is 240°F to 250°F. These high temperatures can only be achieved when using a pressure canner, not a water bather. Pressure canning is the only method of processing that gets food hot enough for long enough, making them safe for long-term storage.

So how will you know which method to use?

A tried-and-true recipe will always have the method and the length of time required for processing. If the recipe does not give you this information, get a different recipe from a reliable source. Each of my recipes have been tested in triplicate using a commercial food grade pH tester.

This method of testing is especially important when canning tomatoes and foods which hover around the 4.6 pH mark. For this reason, I have often changed the method or length of processing time, or added additional acid to the recipe to ensure its safety. A prime example of this is my Basil Diced Tomatoes recipe on page 75. Because this recipe hovered too closely to 4.7pH, it was safest and more efficient to quickly pressure can this recipe rather than process it for a longer time in a water bather.

Does everyone use a pressure canner?

Many countries do not have access to pressure canners and their only option is to water bath everything no matter the recipe's level of acidity. So how is this safely accomplished?

Using the same three pillars (Acidic Value, Time, and Temperature), the processing time is greatly extended, often double to that of a pressure canner's processing time. In these instances, without acid or the ability to achieve 240°F or higher, time is the remaining pillar of safety. Home canning chicken, for example, now requires a processing time of 3 hours when water bathing. This means the home canner must keep the jars fully submerged in boiling water for a full three hours or more depending on their elevation.

The Canning Diva® advocates the use of a pressure canner to get the food's temperature higher keeping the food safer from foodborne pathogens.

Safe Processing Methods

Learn how to tell if your canning lid sealed.

Depending on the elevation or altitude where you live, the rate in which you achieve true temperature when cooking or baking may differ. The same principles apply when home canning.

If you live above 1,000 feet elevation, the atmospheric pressure is reduced, causing water to boil at temperatures lower than 212°F. This is because the atmosphere above 2,500 feet becomes much drier and the air has less oxygen and atmospheric pressure, so cooking, baking, and canning takes longer. It also means water and other liquids evaporate faster and boil at lower temperatures.

When water bathing in a higher elevation, you must increase the processing time to compensate for this difference. When pressure canning, you must increase the pounds of pressure which equivocates to a higher temperature. Home canners must also ensure there is ample water in each vessel to compensate for the faster evaporation in higher elevations.

Here are two simple charts to help you when processing your recipes in higher elevations.

Water Bathing

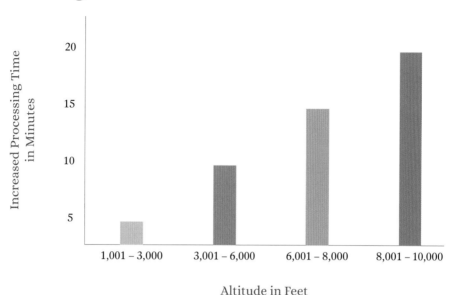

Every canning recipe in *Canning Full Circle* is based on an altitude of less than 1,000 feet, so adjust processing times according to your elevation.

Water bathing is the most popular form of processing for many canners. Because the foods processed in a hot water bath are high in acid, such as jams, salsa, and pickles, we can rely on the temperature of boiling water. To safely process our recipes, the 212°F water temperature must penetrate the contents of each jar, making it imperative each jar is adequately covered with water for the entire duration of the specified processing time.

Here's a quick water bathing tip!

The key is to make sure every jar is fully submerged in water and covered by at least 1-inch of water before processing. If processing jars for more than 15 minutes, be sure jars are fully covered by 2-inches of water to account for evaporation. If after processing, any of the jars are exposed to the air (not covered by water), it is likely harmful bacteria will grow in the exposed food. To remedy this, fully cover the jars with 2-inches of hot water and re-process for the recipe's specified period of time.

Pressure Canning

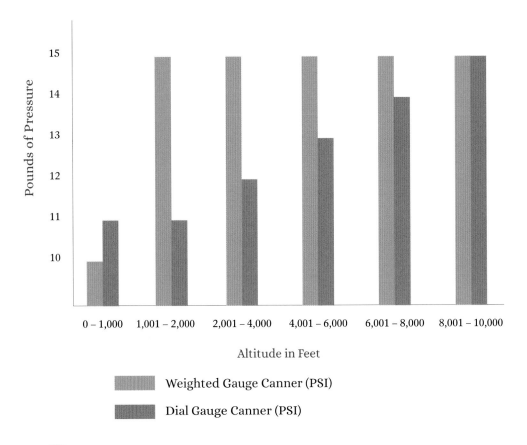

Altitude in Feet

Weighted Gauge Canner (PSI)

Dial Gauge Canner (PSI)

Here's a quick pressure canning tip!

Every canning recipe in *Canning Full Circle* is based on an altitude of less than 1,000 feet, so adjust PSI according to your elevation.

Pressure canning opens the doors for many wonderful foods, meals, and meats to be stored on your pantry shelf! A pressure canner is also a great way to quicken the processing time of high acid foods.

There are two types of stovetop pressure canners: weighted gauge and dial gauge. In recent years, manufacturers have successfully created digital pressure canners specifically designed to process low-acid foods. Pressure canners are designed to use the pressurized air within the vessel to process foods at 240°F and higher, an achievement not possible when water bathing.

When selecting a stovetop pressure canner the smallest size recommended for canning is a 15 ½ quart canner. This size will allow you to process a maximum of

7 quarts or 8 pints at once, depending on the canner manufacturer and type of jar used (wide- or regular-mouth).

When selecting a digital pressure canner, review the manual, often made available online, to ensure the canner was designed to process low-acid foods or if it was created to only water bath high acid foods. Thankfully there are a couple manufacturers who have created a digital canner capable of both water bathing and pressure canning, making it a dual-purpose tool. The trade-off is the digital canner fits less jars than a stovetop canner.

Filling & Sealing Jars

There are several key terms often found in canning recipes. Understanding these terms and properly utilizing their instruction will often be the determining factor as to whether a lid seals or fails. Useful tools such as a headspace measurer and natural bacteria-fighting vinegar are simple, cost-effective ways to substantially decrease lid failures. Properly packing your jars is another key to maximizing yield and utilizing as much jar space as possible.

A quick tip to help prevent lid failures.

Raw-Packing Method

This method is most suitable for vegetables and root crops and also when pickling. Raw-packing is the practice of filling jars tightly with fresh, uncooked food. Hence the term "raw." When using this method, it is common to see foods, especially fruit, floating in the jars. The reason foods may float is due to oxygen becoming trapped within the food, but this is natural and expected.

If during storage food becomes exposed to the trapped oxygen within a sealed jar, it may oxidize, which means the food may slightly darken within 3-6 months of storage. It is still edible, just discolored. This typically happens to the foods not covered by liquids at the very top of the jar and can happen more often when raw-packed.

Hot-Packing Method

Hot-packing is the practice of heating freshly prepared food to boiling, simmering for a specified length of time, then filling the jars with the boiled food. Hot-packing is the best way to remove air trapped within food and is the preferred packing method for foods processed in a water bather. Removing trapped air, or pre-shrinking, allows us to better maximize the jar space.

Additionally, bringing foods to a boil before packing allows a better flavor transfer to blend ingredients so the overall recipe tastes more robust.

Dry-Packing Method

Dry-packing is a newer canning method. This method is typically used when canning root crops such as potatoes. Like traditional raw-packing, the jar is tightly packed with food to maximize yield, however with dry-packing, the food is not covered with boiling water. Instead, the food is coated with a barrier of oil or fat, such as ghee or extra-virgin olive oil, to prevent **oxidiation**. While, oxidiation is a natural occurrence when foods are exposed to air, oxidiation is possible during storage when using this packing method but will not affect the foods safety.

Understanding Headspace

The key to lid sealing starts with a clean jar rim and properly measured **headspace**. Headspace is defined as the unfilled space above the food inside a jar and below its lid. It is crucial to understand and follow the headspace instructions in each recipe. Typically, home canning recipes will specify leaving ¼-inch headspace for jams and jellies, ½-inch headspace for fruits, salsa, chutney and tomatoes, and 1 to 1 ¼-inches in low acidic foods processed in a pressure canner.

The reason headspace is so important when home canning is this open space in each jar is required to give the foods ample space to expand and move during processing. If we fail to give food the space it needs, processing will force the foods out of the jar causing the lid to not seal. We also must have ample headspace to form the required vacuum as the jars cool. This vacuum is how the lid seals to the jar rim and without space to contract, a lid failure is often inevitable.

The extent of expansion is determined by the air content trapped within the food and the required processing time and temperature. Air expands greatly when heated to high temperatures; the higher the temperature and time exposed, the greater the expansion, and therefore the greater the headspace required. For best results, follow the headspace listed in the recipe.

Over-filling jars also prevents the lid from sealing, which is why following proper headspace is crucial when home canning. One of my best examples of this was teaching a canning class how to preserve pie filling in a jar.

The class was instructed to work quickly when stirring the pie filling as it thickens. If left unattended when bringing the pie filling to a boil, it will boil over like an erupting volcano. If the viscosity of the filling acts like this in a stockpot,

Here's an easy way to understand headspace.

imagine what it will do in a jar during a hot water bath. To avoid the pie filling from flowing out of the jars during processing, adhering to a 1 ¼-inch of headspace, also known as a **generous inch headspace**, will give the pie filling room to expand while keeping it in the jar.

So how do you measure headspace? At the base of the headspace measuring tool are notched groves resembling a staircase. Above each notch are embossed measurements from ¼- to 1-inch. Sadly, a headspace measuring tool does not account for a generous inch, so the additional ¼-inch must be eyeballed.

How to Properly Measure Headspace

Using your headspace measuring tool, rest the notch measurement specified in your recipe onto the jar rim and hold upright. Fill your jar until the food touches the tip of the headspace measuring tool. Be sure the tip is not submerged in food – the tip should just touch the food.

If your jar is overfilled, simply use a spoon and remove liquid or food pieces to obtain the proper measurement of headspace. Once the air bubbles are removed and the headspace is properly measured, you may clean your jar rim in preparation for adhering the lids and rings.

Removing Trapped Air

Throughout *Canning Full Circle,* you will see instructions to remove trapped air pockets or air bubbles after filling the jars. Removing trapped air is a crucial step in properly packing jars. The headspace measuring tool doubles as an air bubble remover tool. If you do not own one, you may use a chopstick or the handle on a wooden spoon to remove any trapped air within the jar.

The key to removing trapped air pockets is using your tool around the inside wall of the jar as well as the center mass, being sure to push down foods to release trapped air. If the recipe has a high liquid content, or is raw-packed with large pieces of food, I will often tap the jar gently on a cutting board to agitate its contents to release trapped air. Using a cutting board as a surface will help prevent the glass jar from breaking. When canning foods such as raw chicken, it is essential to lift, move, and push the meat pieces down to ensure the air pockets are released.

Canning with Sugar & Salt

What is the best salt for canning?

There are so many misnomers out there regarding what is required to home can and what truly does the preserving. Often times I hear it is the salt which does the preserving. For this reason, many refrain from home canning because they've been led to believe recipes require more salt than their diet allows. Nothing could be further from the truth. Honestly, controlling what foods go into each jar, including salt, is what makes home canning such a healthy alternative to store bought canned goods.

With the exception of creating brine for pickling recipes, salt when home canning is merely for flavor. As described earlier, it is the acidic value of the foods and the processing method (time and temperature) which preserves our food in jars for long-term storage.

This is also similar for sugar. A misnomer I often hear is that the sugar in jam preserves the fruit. This is not the case. What we do know is a plethora of sugar will help with the gelling abilities when exposed to heat, yet many of us cannot ingest 7 cups of sugar for every batch of strawberry jam.

Using Canning Gel (ClearJel®) to decrease the amount of sugar in jam will increase the berry flavor and thickness while keeping the sugar content low. It is the only thickening agent approved for home canning as it will not impede heat penetration during processing, and it retains viscosity when exposed to high temperatures and acidic foods.

Sugar substitutes approved for home canning are Splenda®, low-glycemic Agave sweetener, and Stevia. Natural sweeteners such as honey and maple syrup may also be used in home canning recipes. Keep in mind, when substituting sugar with Splenda® the recipe will have less liquidity whereas adding Agave, will increase liquidity. All of these options are much sweeter in flavor than traditional sugar.

Thickening Agents

Many canning recipes require a form of thickener whether it's a store-bought powdered pectin, a food starch like Canning Gel (ClearJel®), or finely chopped apples or potatoes.

Pectin, although for the most part is derived from natural ingredients such as apple pulp, in some varieties has limited abilities once exposed to high temperatures for long periods of time. This is often the biggest frustration for first time jam makers. More often than not, the pectin fails to thicken the jam without the use of 7 or more cups of sugar leaving the canner frustrated.

How to use ClearJel® in canning recipes.

Another form of pectin is liquid pectin. This clear, gel-like pectin is essential when making jelly so the finished product should not be translucent in nature. What I have often found when making jelly is the need to double the amount of liquid pectin to get it to gel. Furthermore, the key is timing of its insertion into the recipe to avoid over exposure to high heat so the jelly thickens properly.

Over the years I have perfected what works best with each type of recipe. For instance, the only thickener I will use when canning pie filling is Canning Gel (ClearJel®). It is corn starch mechanically processed down to a fine powder making it perfect for home canning as it can withstand highly acidic foods and extreme temperatures. Without a food starch such as this you will never achieve gorgeous, gooey pie filling.

Adding the Right Type of Acid

Recipe creators understand the three pillars and how they interact. When creating canning recipes, it is important to be aware of the overall acidic value of a recipe to avoid over processing and ruining the foods. It is also important to denature microorganism growth. Increasing the acidic value of a recipe is accomplished in several ways:

Vinegar

There are many types of vinegar used to create recipes. The main two are white vinegar and apple cider vinegar. When purchasing these two types of vinegar, the label must disclose a 5% acidity or higher. If vinegar is diluted, meaning the acidity is less than five percent, your home canned goods will rot overtime during storage.

Vinegar is also an excellent cleaning agent. In home canning, it is used to clean our glass canning jars. This prevents clouding due to mineral deposits from our water. Create a good habit of adding an ounce of vinegar to your canner water prior to processing jars.

Vinegar is also a great way to clean our jar rims prior to adhering a canning lid. The vinegar's properties cut through grease, sugary residue, and food particles which can prevent your lid from sealing.

Bottled Lemon or Lime Juice

Citrus juice is another way to heighten a recipe's acidic value. When home canning, be sure to use store-bought lemon or lime juice, unless the recipe specifically calls for the juice of a fresh lemon or lime.

Bottled citrus juice has a standardized acidic value which keeps the pH consistent. This is required in home canning. The pH of freshly squeezed citrus juice can vary due to where it is harvested, the soil used to grow in, and the type of lemon or lime. When home canning, if freshly squeezed citrus is listed as an ingredient in the recipe it is done so for its flavor, not acidity, and is often accompanied by adding its zest or peel.

When adding small amounts of citrus juice to canning recipes, its flavor is undetectable. For instance, it is recommended when canning tomatoes in water to add bottled citrus juice. This recommendation is due to the plethora of tomato varieties grown throughout the world and their varying pH levels.

Tomato Canning Tip

To increase the acidic value of tomatoes, add 1 tablespoon of bottled lemon juice to every pint jar and 2 tablespoons to every quart jar prior to adding the tomatoes.

Essential Canning Utensils

We have come so far in technology from when I was a kid it just amazes me! Even something as simple and inexpensive as a headspace measuring tool.

Now while we have made many advancements in canning utensils, there are many useless gadgets on the market. I am sure you've seen them – they look awesome on the infomercial but stay tucked in the back of the utensil drawer for decades. We've all been there.

Canning and food preservation is about practicality, so here is a quick list of practical canning essentials that work efficiently and safely.

Stainless Steel Stockpots, Large Colanders, and Bowls

- Select the largest, deepest pot in your kitchen making sure it is not made of a reactive metal such as aluminum, cast iron, or copper. Use stainless steel, ceramic, glass, or enamelware.

- Colanders and bowls should be large enough in size to manage a single batch canning recipe which yields upwards of 7 quarts.

Jars, Lids, and Rings

- Consumers have a wide variety of jar options to choose from when it comes to purchasing them for canning. Jars can be cleaned and reused indefinitely so long as their rim is free of cracks and chips and their base and sides are free of hairline cracks or fractures.

- There are a variety of canning lids on the market now, some even made to be reusable such as Tattler® brand. Rings may be used indefinitely so long as they are not overly rusted.

Keep your rings clean and properly stored.

Headspace Measuring Tool

- This ensures proper headspace in jars for a good lid seal and doubles as an air bubble remover when filling jars. This tool can be purchased with a canning utensil kit or individually.

Wide-Mouth Jar Funnel

- Save time and energy by getting food into the jar the first time. Waste less, can more, and maximize jar space with this effective tool.

Magnetic Lid Grabber

- Get lids in and out of boiling water safely, capturing one lid at a time.

Canning Racks

- Both water bathers and pressure canners require a rack to elevate the glass jars off the heat source. More often than not, the canner will come with one rack. I recommend purchasing a second flat rack if you own a

23-quart or taller pressure canner so you may double stack your jars and increase your output.

Waterproof, Heat-Resistant Canning Mitts, or Jar Grabber

- Dish towels and potholders conduct heat when wet, so having a waterproof mitt or jar grabber keeps you safe by giving you dexterity when handling boiling hot, wet jars.

Tall Mixing Tools and Ladles

- Because we use deep stockpots when canning, having a spoon upwards of 15- to 18-inches tall helps you bring hot foods from the base of the pot to the surface allowing you to properly distribute heat throughout the recipe.

- While many jars can be filled with a ladle, using a tall, slotted spoon will permit you to balance out the ratio of liquids to solids so each jar can stay consistent. This is especially helpful when filling jars for soup recipes.

Dishtowels and Cutting Boards

- Keep hot jars off cold surfaces to avoid fracturing the glass. Dishtowels soak up water and the cutting boards elevate the jars off cold countertops.

Terrycloth Washcloth and Vinegar

- Reserve a separate washcloth solely for wiping jar rims and screw bands. Wiping jar rims with a washcloth dipped in vinegar will remove food debris, kill bacteria, and decrease lid failures.

Reliable Timer and Permanent Marker

- It is essential to track a recipe's cooking time and processing time when placed inside a canner.

- After processing and before storage, jars must be washed and labeled with the recipe name and date it was canned. While adhesive labels are great, a permanent marker does the trick.

These are just a few canning essentials. However, there is nothing wrong with expanding upon this list. For instance, I love wearing an apron but wouldn't consider it essential. When it comes to safety however, I have learned the hard way to protect my hands and face at all costs. For that reason, wearing waterproof heat-resistant canning mitts have become an essential tool in my canning arsenal.

Long-Term Storage

After processing and the jars have cooled and lids have sealed, remove the ring and hand wash the outside of each jar with warm, soapy water. Dry each jar well and label it with the recipe name and the month and year it was preserved. I am often asked if the jars should be stored with their rings on. I do believe it is a personal preference, but here is why I store my jars with the rings off.

Why You Should Store Jars with the Rings Off

One winter when my son was 12 years old, I sent him downstairs to our pantry to get two quarts of home canned Chili con Carne (recipe on page 185). As he approached the top of the stairs, one of the lids literally fell to the floor.

The lid became unsealed during storage, which sometimes, but rarely, happens. We were able to identify this immediately because the jar was stored with the ring off. The ring was not there to create a false impression of a sealed lid.

Let's play this scenario out differently...

Now say I chose to store my home canned goods with the rings on every jar and the lid on that jar of chili became unsealed. My son, being the awesome kid he is, goes downstairs to grab two quarts of Chili con Carne. Arriving at the top of the stairs it goes unnoticed by him that the lid became unsealed during storage because as far as he can tell, it "looks fine." He then takes the initiative to open each jar of chili for me, graciously dumping its contents into the pot to be heated through...and the harmful exposed food goes undetected, and possibly consumed, making us all sick from the bacteria growth.

As rare as it might be, I would much rather have my lid come flying off in transit from the basement to the kitchen, or even on the pantry shelf, than have it go undetected. So, in my home, we store with the rings off. Although that was a dramatic scenario, it happened before my own eyes and reassured me of my decision to store with rings off.

A less dramatic reason to store my home canned goods with the rings off is due to rust. Temperature and humidity fluctuations cause moisture and condensation. Over time, storing with the rings on makes it a blood vessel-popping experience to untwist the ring from the jar and it leaves behind a gross rusty residue on the jar lid and screw bands. Over time, that rust will eat through the lid causing air to enter the jar and rot the food during storage.

Proper Storage Conditions

When storing your home canned goods, here are the ideal conditions:

Stay safe by learning the signs of spoiled food.

1. Temperatures between 50°F and 70°F,
2. A dry area with limited to no humidity or moisture,
3. No direct and indirect sunlight, and
4. Not sitting directly on the floor and certainly not sitting directly on concrete.

I will often keep the bulk of my canned goods in my basement and bring a few jars up to my kitchen cupboards. Keep in mind, storing these soon-to-used jars in the kitchen is fine so long as you do not place them in the cupboard above your refrigerator or stove. The heat generated from appliances will cause the temperature in the cupboard to increase and may also create condensation in air-conditioned rooms.

Easy Storage Locations

There are many other places to store home canned goods other than in a pantry or kitchen cupboard, especially if space is limited.

Some creative areas are
- under your bed,
- in linen closets,
- under stairwells, and
- in a temperature-controlled garage or outbuilding.

Even spare bedrooms have been converted into storage locations with blackout shades covering the cans from direct sunlight. Stacking directly on top of other jars is not recommended because of potential lid failures from the weight or the creation of a false seal.

What is the Shelf-Life of my Home-Canned Foods?

I am often asked, "How long will my home canned food last in storage?" The best way to ensure you are eating your home canned foods at the height of their nutritional value is proper rotation. Get in the habit of remembering this key phrase: *First In, First Out.*

Home canned foods consumed within their first year of preserving are at their optimal nutritional value. Within the second and third year, the foods begin to lose their nutritional value even more. So long as the lid stays sealed and are stored properly, you may get upwards of five years in storage. Keep in mind, some foods may lose texture and darken slightly, but these deteriorations do not affect their safety.

So where does that leave the nutritional aspect?

Those of you who have attended one of my classes, demonstrations, speaking engagements or have followed me online for the last decade have heard me break down the answer like this:

First, I know what I put in every jar. Second, if we can eat Ho Hos, Ding Dongs, and Doritos®, which have limited, if any, real nutritional value, I will gladly eat my home canned foods into year three or more, even if the nutritional value has decreased by more than half.

Working with Glass and High Temperatures

Envision yourself pouring the last cup of hot coffee from your glass coffee pot. Would you race over to the sink and fill the glass pot with ice cold water? No, you sure wouldn't! Because you know doing so would likely cause the glass pot to shatter or severely crack due to the abrupt change in temperature.

When home canning, think of every canning jar as a glass coffee pot. If your jar is packed full of cold foods, the jar should be cold as should the canner water. If the recipe is piping hot, your glass jars should also be hot when filled; and when processing these hot jars, be sure your canner water is also hot.

Remembering the glass coffee pot analogy will keep you safe and your canning jars working for you for years to come!

Start Your Canning Journey

Equipped with the information and tools necessary to start your home canning endeavors, the next step is determining what to preserve in a jar.

My best advice is to

1. Purchase a separate calendar and label it, My Canning Calendar.

2. Find resources in your specific growing area and notate in the calendar when certain produce will be in harvested or plentiful in stores.

3. From this information, start notating which canning recipe you plan to preserve within the food's available time frame. If you are a gardener, you may coincide your canning endeavors with your garden harvest throughout your growing season.

4. Next, select recipes with ingredients you know you and your family enjoy eating. Feel free to get creative but be sure you are selecting foods you know you like. If you wish to be adventurous, simply cut the canning recipe in half and make a smaller, more manageable sized batch. This way, if you do not like the recipe, you have not wasted much time, energy, or food. I've said it before, but I will say it again, "If you won't eat it, don't can it."

5. Lastly, keep in mind, canning is a year-round craft. While spring often means fruit and berries, fall will bring squash and pumpkins. Soups and broths may be made and preserved any time of the year, and never forget fun seasonal favorites and canning specifically for gift-giving.

6. And be sure to freeze meat carcasses and vegetable scraps to later use for broth, stock, and soup making. Using your freezer to store foods until you have time to can them is so helpful!

My last bit of advice…

HAVE FUN!

While there is a great deal of time and effort put into this centuries-old craft, having fun makes all the difference! Grab some friends or your spouse and have a canning party. More hands make lighter work, and you may all share in its bounty.

Whether a novice or veteran canner, the confidence you gain after tackling your fear is life changing. The motivation to preserve more food is amplified with each jar preserved. And the overwhelming sense of pride felt when mastering the art and craft of home canning is the ultimate reward, bringing us back into our kitchens year after year.

So, what are you waiting for?

Happy Canning!

CHAPTER 2

Jams, Butters & Sauces

This chapter explores creative ways to preserve fruit into fun jams, butters, and a variety of sauces. I share with you how to incorporate these home canned treats into amazing meals and desserts.

Apple Cider Butter

MAKES APPROX. 4 PINTS OR 8 HALF-PINTS

This creamy, smooth spread embodies the flavors of fall. Combining apple cider with cinnamon and cloves, takes traditional apple butter from ordinary to extraordinary.

2 cups apple cider

6 pounds apples (18 medium) peeled, cored, and chopped (Use your favorite apple)

1½ teaspoons ground cinnamon

½ teaspoon ground cloves

3 cups raw granulated sugar

Recipe Tip

Have a plate chilling in the refrigerator during recipe prep. Dapple a small amount of apple butter onto the chilled plate. If the butter holds its shape and liquid does not separate from the mixture, your butter is ready to ladle into hot jars.

1 In a large, stainless-steel stockpot, add the apple cider. As you are prepping your apples, place the chopped apples in the stockpot. Give the apples a quick stir so the cider coats the apples to prevent browning.

2 Bring to a boil over medium-high heat. Reduce heat and boil gently for 30 minutes, stirring often to prevent scorching. Apples should be soft.

3 Working in batches, transfer apple mixture to a food processor or food mill and purée. Do not liquefy your apples. Measure 12 cups of apple purée for the recipe.

4 In a thick, wide-bottomed stainless-steel stockpot, combine the apple purée with the spices. Whisk in sugar. Bring to a boil over medium-high heat, stirring frequently to avoid scorching. Once at a boil, reduce heat to low and boil gently to thicken, stirring often. Fruit butters may take anywhere from 30 minutes to an hour to properly thicken.

5 Using a funnel, ladle apple cider butter into hot jars, leaving a ¼-inch of headspace.

6 Remove any air bubbles and add additional apple cider butter if necessary to maintain the ¼-inch of headspace.

7 Wipe the rim of each jar with a warm washcloth dipped in vinegar. Place a lid and ring on each jar and hand-tighten.

8 Place the jars in the water bather, ensuring each jar is covered by at least 1-inch of water. Bring the canner water to a boil on high heat and process half-pints and pints for 10 minutes. Do not start your timer until the canner water is at a full rolling boil. After processing, wait 5 minutes before removing the jars from the canner.

Apple Cider Butter Muffins

MAKES APPROX. 18 MUFFINS

To the Table

What better way to ensure you bake moist and fluffy muffins than by using your home canned Apple Cider Butter. The deep, rich color combined with the sweet, crisp flavor of apple cider creates deliciously flavored muffins. Send a batch to school to celebrate a birthday or simply to put a smile on the teacher's face.

1 ¾ cups flour

1 ½ teaspoons baking powder

1 teaspoon baking soda

¼ teaspoon salt

½ cup softened butter

1 cup raw sugar

1 egg

1 cup home canned Apple Cider Butter

1 teaspoon vanilla extract

5 ounces evaporated milk

1 Preheat oven at 350°F.

2 In a small bowl, stir together the flour, baking powder, baking soda, and salt. Set aside.

3 In a large bowl, combine the butter and sugar. Using a hand beater, beat the ingredients until fluffy. Add the egg to the sugar mixture and mix well.

4 Next, beat in the apple cider butter and vanilla. Alternating between the flour mixture and condensed milk, add the ingredients to the wet mixture until everything is combined. Do not over mix.

5 In greased muffin cups, fill each cup ²/₃ full of muffin mixture. Bake for 20-25 minutes. Remove from oven and let sit for 5 minutes before placing onto a cooling rack.

To the
Jar

Pear Apple Butter

MAKES APPROX. 6 PINTS OR 12 HALF-PINTS

In addition to apples, fall means pears are ripe for the picking. Whether you grow your own or have a local farm nearby, using pears to heighten the flavor of your apple butter is a total game changer. This beautiful butter turns a gorgeous red hue and is naturally sweet. Excellent in a yogurt parfait, a Danish pastry, or use a half-pint jar to glaze a ham. No matter its use, this butter is sure to please.

6 pounds pears (18 medium), seeded and quartered

4 pounds apples (12 medium), cored, seeded and quartered

1 cup granulated sugar

1 tablespoon ground cinnamon (optional)

1 teaspoon ground nutmeg (optional)

1 In a large, thick-bottomed stockpot, combine the pears and apples. Bring to a boil over medium-high heat, stirring frequently. Reduce the heat to low and simmer for 20 minutes, or until the fruit becomes soft. Remove from heat and let cool enough to handle.

2 Working in batches, run the fruit mixture through a food mill. Discard peels and transfer the fruit mixture to a clean thick-bottomed stockpot or slow cooker crockpot. Add the granulated sugar and cinnamon and nutmeg, if using. Mix well.

3 Slowly cook the fruit mixture for 1 hour on low heat on the stovetop, stirring occasionally, or for 6 hours on low in the slow cooker crockpot. Cook down to let moisture evaporate and thicken the butter.

4 Using a funnel, ladle the hot pear apple butter into jars leaving a ¼-inch of headspace. Remove any air bubbles and add additional butter if necessary to maintain the ¼-inch headspace.

5 Wipe the rim of each jar with a clean washcloth dipped in vinegar. Place a lid and ring on each jar and hand-tighten.

6 Place the jars in the water bather, ensuring each jar is covered by at least 1-inch of water. Bring the canner to a boil on high heat and process half-pints and pints for 10 minutes. Do not start your timer until the water is at a full rolling boil. After processing, wait 5 minutes before removing the jars from the canner.

Peach Pistachio Conserve

MAKES APPROX. 3 PINTS OF 6 HALF-PINTS

I had so much fun creating this recipe! I brought a couple jars to my aunt Maggie's house for taste-testing! Our results: this flavorful conserve is delicious atop goat cheese, complements Foie gras beautifully, and makes an excellent addition to a Prosciutto and Pancetta plate. Enhance its flavors by sprinkling a touch of Himalayan sea salt prior to serving!

2 cups unsalted, shelled pistachio nuts, chopped

4 cups peaches, peeled and finely chopped (approx. 8 peaches)

2 cups sweet cherries, pitted and coarsely chopped

Zest and juice from 2 large oranges

2 cups golden raisins

1 tablespoon fresh gingerroot, grated

¼ cup fresh mint, finely chopped

2 tablespoons lemon juice

6 tablespoons Canning Gel

1 Pistachio Prep: In the event you cannot procure unsalted nuts, place salted pistachios in a colander in the sink and rinse thoroughly until the salt has been removed. Simply pat pistachios dry before chopping.

2 In a large, stainless-steel stockpot, combine the pistachios, peaches, cherries, orange juice and zest, golden raisins, gingerroot, mint, and lemon juice. Bring to a boil over medium-high heat. Stir constantly to avoid scorching.

3 Once at a boil, reduce heat and whisk in Canning Gel. Boil gently for 10 minutes, stirring frequently to avoid scorching as the conserve thickens.

4 Using a funnel, ladle hot conserve into jars leaving a ¼-inch of headspace. Remove any air bubbles and add additional conserve if necessary to maintain the ¼-inch headspace.

5 Wipe the jar rim with a warm washcloth dipped in vinegar. Place a lid and ring on each jar and hand-tighten.

6 Place the jars in the water bather, ensuring each jar is covered by at least 1-inch of water. Bring the canner water to a boil on high heat and process half-pints for 15 minutes and pints for 20 minutes. Do not start your timer until the canner water is at a full rolling boil. After processing, wait 5 minutes before removing the jars from the canner.

Charcuterie Plate

APPROX. 4 TO 6 SERVINGS

This crowd-pleasing hors d'oeuvre can often be seen at high-end restaurants, but now you can enjoy it in your own home with just a few, fun tips from The Canning Diva®. Wow your guests with the addition of Peach Pistachio Conserve to your next Charcuterie Board.

The real fun begins with a variety of cured and thinly sliced cuts of meat. Be sure to purchase at least 2-3 ounces of meat per person when shopping.

Sausages – smoked chorizo or saucisson sec are popular favorites along with a cooked garlic sausage

Paper-thin Muscle Cuts – a cured pork tenderloin like lomo or cured beef tenderloin like bresaola

Smoked Country Hams – Prosciutto offers many varieties like Jambon de Bayonne, a French prosciutto or something fun like duck or boar prosciutto

Cheese, Fruits & Nuts

1 pint jar of Peach Pistachio Conserve

1 pint jar of Pickled Garlic Cloves (page 163)

1 cup blonde raisins

2 tablespoons raw honey

Thinly sliced Swiss Cheese, Havarti, and aged Cheddar cheese

1 medium size gingerroot

6-8 ounces Brie cheese

Himalayan sea salt

1 baguette cut into 1-inch thick slices or 1 box of peppered rice crackers

1 Grab your favorite serving platter or use a large wooden cutting board. Taking each slice of meat, lightly fold and drape across each other into a decorative elongated pile, keeping the various meats grouped accordingly. Place the cheese slices in groups alongside the meats. Peel the exterior of the ginger root to unveil the fresh center. In long, firm strokes, peel enough zesty strips so your guests have at least two each.

2 Fill a container with your Peach Pistachio Conserve and another with your Pickled Garlic Cloves. Create a pile of raisins off to one side, smear the honey off into one corner, place the ginger strips in another, and cut the Brie into ¼-inch thick slices and pile alongside the sliced baguette. There's no wrong way to create a Charcuterie Board – so have some fun with it!

Peach Pistachio Cobbler

To the Table

MAKES APPROX. 8 TO 10 SERVINGS

Need a quick dessert in under an hour? Use your Peach Pistachio Conserve and serve a scrumptious cobbler – straight from the jar and into the oven. The combination of fruity flavors and crunchy pistachios bake into gooey yumminess while the golden-brown dough compliments it beautifully.

3 pints Peach Pistachio Conserve

2 cups all-purpose flour

¼ cup granulated sugar

2 teaspoons baking powder

½ teaspoon salt

½ teaspoon ground cinnamon

12 tablespoons cold unsalted butter, cut into small cubes

½ cup buttermilk (whole milk may also be used)

1 teaspoon vanilla extract

1 Preheat oven to 375°F. Prepare a 9x13 baking dish by coating it with nonstick cooking spray or a light layer of Crisco®.

2 Add Peach Pistachio Conserve to the baking dish and evenly distribute.

Place baking dish in the oven on the middle rack and bake for 10 minutes.

3 Meanwhile, in a large bowl add flour, sugar, baking powder, salt, and cinnamon. Whisk the ingredients together. Add the cubed butter. Using a pastry cutter, cut butter into the dry ingredients until the butter is no larger than a pea. Using a rubber spatula, scrape all the mixture off the sides of the bowl and create a well in the center.

4 Using a liquid measuring cup, combine the buttermilk and vanilla extract and whisk together. Pour into the well in the center of the dough. Fold together using the rubber spatula until the dough comes together. Do not overwork the dough, keep it lumpy.

5 Remove the conserve from the oven and carefully add the dough by placing small spoonfuls all over the conserve. It is okay if not every area of the conserve is covered and there are open spaces. Return the baking dish to the oven on the middle rack.

6 Bake for 45 minutes or until the conserve is bubbling and the dough is golden brown. Remove from the oven and let rest 20 minutes before serving (ideally with a scoop of vanilla ice cream!).

Less Sugar Berry Jam

MAKES APPROX. 2 PINTS OR 5 HALF-PINTS

Once you experience a homemade jam, it's rare you'll buy a store-bought version again! This recipe is great for those who cannot ingest the high volumes of sugar used in standard jam recipes, but still want a sweet spread for their food.

Canning Gel, or ClearJel®, is a natural thickener permitting canners to drastically decrease the sugar content without losing the jam's gelling abilities. Feel free to double or triple the recipe when canning.

4 cups crushed berries (2 quarts fresh)

¼ cup lemon juice

7 tablespoons Canning Gel

1 ½ to 2 cups granulated sugar, divided

1 Using a colander, clean your berries being sure to remove any stems and suspect berries. In a medium sized bowl, working in batches, use a potato masher and crush the berries. Measure crushed berries and some of their juice. Continue this process until a full 4 cups is achieved.

2 Place crushed berries in a thick-bottomed stainless steel stockpot. Add lemon juice and stir.

3 Using a whisk, mix the Canning Gel into ¼ cup of the sugar. Add sugar mixture to the berries. Bring contents to a boil over medium-high heat and stir constantly. Add remaining sugar. Boil for 1 minute. Remove from heat.

4 Using a funnel, ladle the jam into hot jars leaving a ¼-inch of headspace. Remove any air bubbles and add additional jam if necessary to maintain the ¼-inch headspace.

5 Wipe the rim of each jar with a clean washcloth dipped in vinegar. Place a lid and ring on each jar and hand-tighten.

6 Place jars in the water bather, ensuring each jar is covered by at least 1-inch of water. Bring the canner to a boil and process half-pints for 10 minutes and pints for 15 minutes. Do not start your timer until the water is at a full rolling boil. After processing, wait 5 minutes before removing the jars from the canner.

Blackberry Peach Jam

MAKES APPROX. 2 PINTS OR 5 HALF-PINTS

You will be amazed by this combination of fruit and berry! Using the less sugar jam premise, this delicious jam boasts unbelievable flavors that will jump-start your taste buds. The sweet tones from the peach balance the tartness of the blackberries. Perfect for a PB&J sandwich or in the center of a cupcake, the uses are limitless.

4 cups crushed blackberries

1 large peach, pitted and peeled

¼ cup lemon juice

7 tablespoons Canning Gel

1 to 1 ½ cups sugar

1 Using a colander, clean your berries being sure to remove any stems and suspect berries. In a medium sized bowl, working in batches, use a potato masher and crush the berries. Measure crushed berries and some of their juice. Continue this process until a full 4 cups is achieved. Place crushed blackberries in a stockpot.

2 Chop the peeled peach into small chunks and add it to the blackberries then crush the peaches and blackberries together using a potato masher, purposely seeking out the peach chunks and mashing them.

3 Place crushed fruit mixture in a thick-bottomed stainless-steel stockpot. Add lemon juice and stir.

4 Using a whisk, mix the Canning Gel into ¼ cup of the sugar. Add sugar mixture to the berries. Bring contents to a boil on medium-high heat, and stir constantly. Add remaining sugar. Bring back to a boil. Set timer and boil for 1 minute. Remove from heat.

5 Ladle the jam into hot jars leaving a ¼-inch of headspace. Remove any air bubbles and add additional jam if necessary to maintain the ¼-inch headspace.

6 Using a warm washcloth dipped in vinegar, wipe jar rims and screw bands. Place sterilized lids and rings atop each jar and hand tighten.

7 Place the jars in the water bather, ensuring each jar is covered by at least 1-inch of water. Bring the canner to a boil on high heat and process half-pints for 10 minutes and pints for 15 minutes. Do not start your timer until the water is at a full rolling boil. After processing, wait 5 minutes before removing the jars from the canner.

Grandma Gould's Green Tomato Jam

To the Jar

MAKES APPROX. 4 PINTS OR 8 HALF-PINTS

Every year Grandma Gould relished knowing not every tomato would ripen, leaving these green tart beauties for her favorite jam. Beautiful green tomatoes are sweetened and seasoned making this jam simply delicious. Spread over piping hot corn bread, add to your next charcuterie board, accompany any breakfast dish, or use as a replacement for ketchup.

6 pounds green tomatoes (24 small), cored and finely chopped (8 cups)

5 cups granulated sugar

¼ teaspoon ground cinnamon

1 teaspoon vanilla extract

1 lemon, halved and thinly sliced, seeded

Ingredient Tip

Want to give this sweet jam some zing? Grate a 3-inch piece of peeled gingerroot, totaling 3 tablespoons, and add it to the jam when cooking down the green tomatoes. Need some heat? Add 1 tablespoon of red pepper flakes when adding the vanilla and lemon slices.

1 Add tomatoes, sugar, and cinnamon to a thick-bottomed stainless steel stockpot. Bring to a boil over medium-high heat and boil for 30 minutes, stirring frequently to avoid scorching.

2 Reduce heat to low and simmer. Add vanilla extract and lemon slices. Stirring frequently, cook for an additional 30-45 minutes or until the jam begins to thicken.

3 Using a funnel, ladle jam into hot jars leaving a ¼-inch headspace. Remove any air bubbles and add additional jam if necessary to maintain the ¼-inch headspace.

4 Wipe the rim of each jar with a clean washcloth dipped in vinegar. Place a lid and ring on each jar and hand-tighten.

5 Place the jars in the water bather, ensuring each jar is covered by at least 1-inch of water. Bring the canner to a boil on high heat and process half-pints and pints for 20 minutes. Do not start your timer until the water is at a full rolling boil. After processing, wait 5 minutes before removing the jars from the canner.

Adobo Sauce

MAKES APPROX. 6 HALF-PINTS OR 12 QUARTER-PINTS

The secret sauce used to create so many authentic Mexican and Tex-Mex recipes will now grace your pantry shelf. This amazing sauce is made using chili powder from dried poblanos combined with smoked jalapeño, known as chipotle peppers. Inspired by my friend and canning enthusiast, Vicki Neal.

18 -24 dried chipotle peppers

3 cups boiling water

1 cup Ancho chili powder

5-6 Roma tomatoes (2 ½ cups)

8 garlic cloves

½ cup apple cider vinegar

¼ cup brown sugar

1 tablespoon ground cumin

2 teaspoons dried oregano

1 teaspoon salt

½ teaspoon cinnamon

¼ teaspoon ground allspice

¼ teaspoon ground black pepper

Ingredient Tip

Don't have access to Ancho chili powder? No worries. Use the same chili powder called for when making a batch of chili con carne and add 1 tablespoon of crushed red pepper flakes. This blend of spices will taste just as delicious and give the sauce a bit of heat.

1 Remove the stem end of each chipotle pepper and place in a stockpot cover with water. Bring it to a boil over medium-high heat. Reduce heat to low, cover, and simmer for 40 minutes. Remove from heat.

2 Using a blender or food processor, add the boiling water, chili powder, tomatoes, garlic cloves, vinegar, sugar, cumin, oregano, salt, cinnamon, allspice, and black pepper and purée until smooth. Or add ingredients to a saucepan and purée using an emulsion blender.

3 Transfer sauce to a thick bottomed saucepan and bring to a boil on medium-high heat. Reduce heat to simmer. Cook sauce down for 30 minutes, stirring often to avoid scorching.

4 Using tongs, remove rehydrated chipotle peppers from the hot water and 1-2 peppers in each quarter pint. Place 3 to 4 peppers into each half-pint jar process half-and quarter-pints for 25 minutes.

5 Using a funnel, ladle hot sauce over top the rehydrated peppers in each jar, filling to a ½-inch of headspace. Remove any trapped air pockets and add additional sauce if necessary to maintain the ½-inch headspace.

6 Wipe the rim of each jar with a clean washcloth dipped in vinegar. Place a lid and ring on each jar and hand-tighten.

7 Place the jars in the water bather, ensuring each jar is covered by at least 1-inch of water. Bring the canner to a boil on high heat and process half-pints for 25 minutes. Do not start your timer until the water is at a full rolling boil. After processing, wait 5 minutes before removing the jars from the canner.

To the Table

Tomatillo Chicken

MAKES APPROX. 5 SERVINGS

Make an amazing meal using the peppers from your home canned Adobo Sauce, fresh tomatillos, and potatoes. The recipe can even be scaled up or down to meet the size of your family or guests.

4 tablespoons olive or avocado oil

2 teaspoons salt

½ teaspoon black pepper

5 chicken thighs

5 chicken legs

20 tomatillos, dehusked and cut into ½-inch cubes

4 medium Yukon Gold potatoes, ½-inch cubes

1 cup diced white onion

1 cup corn kernels

2 tablespoons minced garlic

½ bunch fresh cilantro, finely chopped

1 chipotle pepper in Adobo sauce, finely chopped

2 teaspoons dried oregano

4 cups chicken or vegetable broth

1 Using a Dutch oven or deep skillet, heat oil on medium-high heat. Salt and pepper both sides of the chicken and add the chicken skin side down into the hot oil. Brown the chicken for 8 to 10 minutes, then flip and brown for an additional 5 minutes. Remove the chicken from the pan and set aside to rest. If using pork, see the Tip below.

2 In the same skillet, add the tomatillos, potatoes, onion, corn, garlic, cilantro, chipotle peppers, and oregano. Mix well and cook for 5 to 8 minutes, stirring occasionally, until onions are translucent.

3 Add the chicken broth and mix well. Bring the mixture to a quick boil, then reduce heat to medium. Add browned chicken, skin side up, in a single layer being sure not to submerge the chicken. Reduce heat to medium-low and simmer, uncovered, for 30 minutes or until sauce has thickened.

4 When serving, place the tomatillo potato mixture onto the plate first, then place a thigh and leg atop the pile. Feel free to sprinkle freshly chopped cilantro atop the plate before serving.

Ingredient Tip

Don't have tomatillos handy? Use two 11-ounce cans of store-bought green tomatillos to make this dish. If you prefer to use pork instead of chicken, you may use a small pork loin or 5-8 pork chops (boneless or bone-in) to create this dish.

Blueberry BBQ Sauce

MAKES APPROX. 4 PINTS OR 8 HALF-PINTS

Add a punch of flavor to your favorite dishes with this amazing blueberry inspired BBQ sauce. Baste it on pork tenderloin or smoked ribs, slather onto grilled chicken drumsticks or atop your favorite burger patty with a slice of bacon. It even pairs beautifully with fish.

10 cups whole blueberries, crushed

Zest and juice from 1 lime

5 cups sugar

1 cup brown sugar

1 cup apple cider vinegar

1 cup water

¾ cup tomato paste (6 ounces)

1 tablespoon soy sauce

Ingredient Tip

Wish to add a bit of heat to your sauce? Add 2 teaspoons of red pepper flakes or 1 finely diced jalapeño at the start of the recipe. The sweet and hot combination will give any recipe a one, two kick!

1 In a deep saucepan, combine crushed blueberries, the juice of one lime and its grated zest, sugar, brown sugar, apple cider vinegar, and water. Bring to a boil over medium-high heat. Then, reduce heat to low and simmer for 5 minutes.

2 Add tomato paste and soy sauce and mix well. Continue to simmer for an additional 5 minutes, stirring frequently.

3 Using a funnel, ladle sauce into hot jars filling to a ½-inch headspace. Remove any trapped air pockets and add additional sauce if necessary to maintain the ½-inch headspace.

4 Wipe the rim of each jar with a clean washcloth dipped in vinegar. Place a lid and ring on each jar and hand-tighten.

5 Place the jars in the water bather, ensuring each jar is covered by at least 1-inch of water. Bring the canner to a boil on high heat and process half-pints and pints for 15 minutes. Do not start your timer until the water is at a full rolling boil. After processing, wait 5 minutes before removing the jars from the canner.

 **To the Jar**

Roasted Tomato Pizza Sauce

MAKES APPROX. 10 PINTS OR 20 HALF-PINTS

Get ready for the best homemade pizza sauce you've ever canned. The depth of flavor from roasting tomatoes with amazing fresh herbs sets this sauce apart. Use when making homemade pizzas, stovetop chili, a baked egg skillet, and so much more.

90 Roma tomatoes, cored

3 heads of garlic

2 tablespoons olive oil

½ cup brown sugar

1 cup fresh basil leaves, coarsely chopped

¼ cup fresh oregano leaves

¼ cup fresh thyme leaves

3 tablespoons salt

1 tablespoon dried, crushed rosemary

1 tablespoon dried marjoram

1 teaspoon black pepper

½ teaspoon rubbed sage

1/8 cup lemon juice

1 Preheat oven to 425°F.

2 Clean and core your tomatoes. Using a pairing knife, slice 2 to 3 lengthwise slits into the skin of each tomato. Place the tomatoes on a rimmed cookie sheet. Roast in oven until the tomatoes are slightly charred and the skins are lifting from the tomatoes, about 30 to 45 minutes.

3 Cut off the top of each garlic head. Place all three cut heads of garlic into a small baking dish, or ramekins, drizzle with olive oil and roast until garlic cloves are golden brown and soft, about 25 to 35 minutes.

4 After roasting the tomatoes and garlic, set aside until cool to touch. Remove as much of the tomato skin as possible and discard. Place tomatoes in a large stockpot.

5 Holding the base of the garlic head, squeeze until each clove slips out. Place roasted garlic cloves into the stockpot with the tomatoes.

6 Bring the tomatoes to a boil over medium high heat, mashing with a potato masher as they soften. Boil for 30 minutes, stirring and mashing often.

7 Purée tomatoes; work in batches using a food processor or emulsion blender.

8 Add brown sugar, basil, oregano, thyme, salt, rosemary, marjoram, black pepper, sage, and lemon juice to the tomatoes and mix well. Return the sauce to a boil, then reduce heat and simmer, stirring often to avoid scorching. Simmer and stir for one hour or until sauce thickens to desired consistency.

9 Using a funnel, ladle the pizza sauce into hot jars leaving a ½-inch of headspace. Remove any trapped air pockets and add additional pizza sauce if necessary to maintain the ½-inch headspace.

10 Wipe the rims of each jar with a washcloth dipped in vinegar. Place a lid and ring on each jar and hand-tighten.

11 Place the jars in the water bather, ensuring each jar is covered by at least 2-inches of water. Bring the canner to a boil on high heat and process half-pints and pints for 35 minutes. Do not start your timer until the water is at a full rolling boil. After processing, wait 5 minutes before removing the jars from the canner.

Easy Braised Beef Dinner

To the Table

MAKES APPROX. 4 TO 6 SERVINGS

This seared beef one-pot meal is the perfect solution to a chilly fall day. Using two pints of Roasted Tomato Pizza Sauce and a jar of home canned Mirepoix makes meal prep simple. So, grab your Dutch oven and head to your pantry – dinner is made easy tonight.

3 tablespoons vegetable oil

4 pounds boneless beef chuck roast, cut into 2-inch chunks

Salt and pepper

2 pints of Mirepoix (page 68)

1 pint Roasted Tomato Pizza Sauce

3 tablespoons all-purpose flour

1 cup red wine, Pinot Noir or Cabernet

3 cups loosely packed fresh Cremini mushrooms, cut in half

2 bay leaves

Ingredient Tip

If you have not home canned Mirepoix and wish to make this recipe, simply use the following ingredients: 2 tablespoons minced garlic, 2 cups diced yellow onions, 4 large carrots (peeled and chopped), and 1 stalk of celery, finely chopped.

1 Preheat oven to 350°F.

2 Heat oil in a large Dutch oven on the stovetop using medium-high heat. After cutting beef into chunks, pat dry with a paper towel and season with salt and pepper. Working in batches, place beef chunks into the Dutch oven and brown meat on all sides. After browning, remove beef chunks and set aside in clean bowl.

3 Add Mirepoix and pizza sauce to the Dutch oven on a medium-high heat, stirring and scraping up bits from the bottom of the Dutch oven.

4 Sprinkle flour into sauce and stir until absorbed. Stir in the wine and add the mushrooms and bay leaves. Stir to combine.

5 Add beef chunks in a single layer, resting them just above the liquid line, do not submerge them in the sauce.

6 Place the cover on the Dutch oven and put in center of oven. Cook for 2 ½ to 3 hours. Meat should gently fall apart with a fork when done.

7 Serve over top mashed potatoes with a side salad and fresh bread.

CHAPTER 3

Fruit, Legumes & Vegetables

Who would have thought easy home canned staples could be preserved to create scrumptious dishes like ravioli, hummus, cake, and pie. In this chapter, we have fun exploring creative concepts to help make meals easy and delicious.

Sweet Potatoes

MAKES APPROX. 7 QUARTS OR 14 PINTS

There are many fun reasons to have this healthy potato on the ready. Home canned sweet potato makes an excellent side dish when whipped together with cream and dried sage. They also create a delicious sweet potato pie in a sinch.

18 pounds sweet potatoes (about 48 medium), peeled and cubed

5 quarts water (20 cups)

1 Place cubed sweet potatoes into a large stainless steel stockpot and cover with water. Bring to a boil over medium-high heat. Boil for 10 minutes then remove from heat and drain.

2 In another stockpot, bring 5 quarts of water to a boil then shut off heat.

3 Using a funnel, hot pack drained sweet potatoes tightly into jars leaving a 1-inch headspace. Ladle fresh boiling water over potatoes being sure to keep the 1-inch headspace. Remove air pockets by lightly tapping the jar onto a cutting board. Add additional water if necessary to maintain a 1-inch headspace.

4 Wipe the rim of each jar with a clean washcloth dipped in vinegar. Place a lid and ring on each jar and hand-tighten.

5 Place the jars in the pressure canner filled with 3 quarts of water, lock the pressure canner lid, and bring the canner to a boil on high heat. Let the canner vent for 10 minutes. Process at 10 psi or according to your canner type and elevation. Process quarts for 90 minutes and pints for 65 minutes.

6 Allow canner to return to zero psi before removing the canner lid. Wait 5 minutes before removing the jars from the canner.

Sweet Potato Ravioli

MAKES APPROX. 4 SERVINGS

To the Table

This fall favorite dinner is made simple by using your home canned sweet potato. Simply drain, season, and whip together to create a delicious dinner. Wow your guests any time of the year with other pasta fillings like tortellini pasta dumplings, cappelletti, and even sage sausage and sweet potato stuffed manicotti. Make your own pasta or purchase pre-made at the store.

2 pints Sweet Potatoes, drained

1 cup ricotta cheese

¼ cup grated Parmesan cheese

1 egg yolk

1 tablespoon rubbed sage

½ teaspoon salt

⅛ teaspoon black pepper

Create your own dough or use store bought wanton wrappers

1 egg set aside for sealing ravioli

1 Add the drained sweet potatoes to a large mixing bowl and mash with a fork or potato masher until the consistency is even and thick. Add ricotta cheese, parmesan cheese, egg yolk, sage, salt, and pepper. Mix well until evenly blended. Cover bowl with plastic wrap and place in refrigerator to chill for 30 minutes.

2 While the filling chills, either make your own ravioli pasta dough and cut with a mold, or use store-bought wonton wrappers.

3 Crack one egg into a small bowl and add 2 teaspoons of water. Whisk well and set aside.

4 Fill the center of the ravioli dough or wonton wrapper with 1 ½ to 2 teaspoons of sweet potato filling. Dip a pastry brush into the whisked egg mixture and lightly brush the edges of each ravioli or wonton wrapper before encasing the filling.

5 Boil ravioli in a pot of boiling water for about 3 minutes. Drain well and serve.

Recipe Tip

For a delicious brown butter sauce, brown 4 ounces of butter. Then, flavor with fresh sage, finely chopped shallots, red pepper flakes, and pecans or pine nuts. Toss the boiled ravioli in the sauce before serving hot.

Canning Aromatics

MAKES APPROX. 5 PINTS OR 10 HALF-PINTS

ASIAN TRINITY MAKES APPROX. 5 HALF-PINTS

Aromatics is a term used to describe a traditional group of vegetables which are the foundational base of flavors to a particular cuisine. Many recipes are created using essentials like carrots, onions, and peppers with varying degrees of heat. Give depth to your home cooked meals by preserving these common aromatic combinations.

French Mirepoix

2 large onions, diced (4 cups)

1 pound (about 9 medium) carrots, peeled and chopped (3 cups)

6 celery stalks, diced (3 cups)

Cajun Holy Trinity

2 large onions, diced (4 cups)

6 celery stalks, diced (3 cups)

3 medium bell peppers, chopped (3 cups)

Italian Soffritto

2 large onions, diced (4 cups)

1 pound (about 9 medium) carrots, peeled and chopped (3 cups)

6 celery stalks, diced (3 cups)

5 tablespoons parsley, coarsely chopped

Latin Sofrito

2 large onions, diced (4 cups)

3 medium bell peppers, chopped (3 cups)

6 Roma tomatoes, diced (3 cups)

5 tablespoons minced garlic

Asian Trinity

8 bunches scallions, diced (4 cups)

10 tablespoons gingerroot, peeled and chopped fine

5 tablespoons minced garlic

1 Place each prepared ingredient for the specific Aromatic Cuisine in a separate bowl.

2 The recipe is raw stacked, which means each ingredient is evenly distributed and layered in the jar raw. Starting with the onions, evenly distribute diced onions amongst each pint jar, about ¾ cup per pint or $\frac{1}{3}$ cup per half-pint.

3 Next, evenly distribute and layer any remaining vegetables in the aromatic recipe such as carrots, celery, peppers or tomatoes. Place about a ½ cup of each remaining vegetable per pint and $\frac{1}{3}$ cup per half-pint. Lastly, if your aromatic recipe requires a fresh herb or minced garlic, evenly distribute amongst each jar.

4 Cover aromatics with cool water, leaving a 1-inch headspace. Gently tap the jar on a cutting board to release trapped air. Add additional water if necessary to maintain a 1-inch headspace.

5 Wipe the rim of each jar with a warm washcloth dipped in vinegar. Place a lid and ring on each jar and hand tighten.

6 Place jars in pressure canner filled with 3 quarts of cool water, lock the pressure canner lid, and warm the canner on medium heat for 10 minutes. After canner has warmed, bring the canner to a boil on high heat. Let the canner vent for 10 minutes. Process at 10 psi or according to your canner type and elevation. Process pints and half-pints for 25 minutes.

7 Allow canner to return to zero psi before removing the canner lid. Wait 5 minutes before removing the jars from the canner.

The Canning Divas

70

Vegetable Medley

MAKES APPROX. 7 QUARTS OR 14 PINTS

The perfect array of vegetables giving you aide in the kitchen when creating meals. Use this delicious mixture as the base to vegetable pot pie filling, or when starting a batch of vegetable soup on the stovetop. This medley also makes an easy side dish to any main course.

2 ½ pounds (18 medium) carrots, peeled and chopped (6 cups)

6 cups corn kernels, fresh or frozen

6 cups shelled peas, fresh or frozen

1 ½ pounds green beans, fresh or frozen, trimmed and cut into 1-inch pieces (6 cups)

5 medium russet potatoes, cut into ½ inch cubes (5 cups)

6 celery stalks, chopped (3 cups)

7 teaspoons salt (optional)

1 Add carrots, corn, peas, green beans, potatoes, and celery to a large stainless steel stockpot and add enough water to cover. Bring to a boil over medium-high heat, mixing frequently to avoid scorching.

2 Boil for 5 minutes, then remove from heat.

3 Using a funnel, ladle hot vegetables into jars, leaving a 1-inch headspace. If using salt, add 1 teaspoon to each quart and ½ teaspoon to each pint jar. Remove any air bubbles and add additional liquid to maintain headspace.

4 Place the jars in the pressure canner filled with 3 quarts of water, lock the pressure canner lid, and bring the canner to a boil on high heat. Let the canner vent for 10 minutes. Process at 10 psi or according to your canner type and elevation. Process quarts for 90 minutes and pints for 75 minutes.

5 Allow canner to return to zero psi before removing the canner lid. Wait 5 minutes before removing the jars from the canner.

Ingredient Tip

This is the perfect recipe to use up frozen vegetables and create more space in your freezer. You may also add additional seasonings to each jar such as black pepper, minced garlic, ginger, basil leaves, and thyme.

Dry Packed Potatoes with Peppers & Onions

To the Jar

MAKES APPROX. 12 QUARTS OR 24 PINTS

This recipe makes the BEST fried potatoes on the planet! Say goodbye to soggy potatoes and 3 inches of starch when stored in water. Simply open a jar and empty into a cast iron skillet and fry until golden brown. Makes an excellent addition to any breakfast or dinner.

30 pounds potatoes, scrubbed clean and cut into 1-inch cubes (peeling optional)

5 large bell peppers, diced (7 ½ cups)

2 large sweet onions, diced (4 cups)

5 tablespoons minced garlic

½ cup melted butter or ghee

Ingredient Tip

Instead of butter or ghee, you may coat your ingredients with ¼ cup extra-virgin olive oil. You may also cut your potatoes into uniform shaped wedges or into larger 2-inch chunks.

1 Thoroughly scrub your potatoes with a vegetable brush under running water. It is okay if some of the skin scrubs off. Be sure to remove any dry rot, eyes or sprouts from the potato's exterior. After scrubbing the entire potato well, rinse again in fresh running water. You may also peel your potatoes if you do not desire the skins be left on.

2 In a large stockpot, combine cubed potatoes, peppers, onions, and minced garlic. Mix well to thoroughly coat. Cover mixture with melted butter or ghee. If using olive oil, refer to the Ingredient Tip.

3 Using a funnel, fill jars and pack tight, tapping everything down as you add more vegetables. Fill to a 1-inch headspace.

4 Wipe the rim of each jar with a clean washcloth dipped in vinegar. Place a lid and ring on each jar and hand-tighten.

5 Place the jars in the pressure canner filled with 3 quarts of cool water, lock the pressure canner lid, and warm the canner on medium heat for 10 minutes. After canner has warmed, bring the canner to a boil on high heat. Let the canner vent for 10 minutes. Process at 10 psi or according to your canner type and elevation. Process quarts for 40 minutes and pints for 35 minutes.

6 Allow canner to return to zero psi before removing the canner lid. Wait 5 minutes before removing the jars from the canner.

Basil Diced Tomatoes

MAKES APPROX. 4 QUARTS OR 8 PINTS

Need an alternative to stewed tomatoes? Give my Basil Diced Tomatoes a try. Slices of garlic, fresh basil leaves, and a touch of black pepper make these the most versatile tomato in your pantry. Use Basil Diced Tomatoes in soups, stews, or over baked chicken. Sometimes I'll just heat up a jar and toss with pasta if I'm not in the mood for a heavy sauce. The possibilities are endless!

16 cups diced Roma tomatoes

1 large yellow (or green) bell pepper, chopped

1 large onion, chopped

¼ cup fresh, coarsely chopped basil

2 tablespoons minced garlic

2 tablespoons salt

1 tablespoon sugar

Fresh ground black pepper to taste

8 tablespoons bottled lemon juice

1 In a large, stainless steel stockpot, combine tomatoes, yellow bell pepper, onions, basil leaves, garlic, salt, sugar, and pepper and bring to a boil over medium-high heat. Reduce heat to medium and boil gently for 5 minutes, stirring often.

2 Add 2 tablespoons of bottled lemon juice to each quart jar or 1 tablespoon of bottled lemon juice to each pint jar.

3 Using a funnel and slotted spoon, add tomato mixture to each jar filling to a generous 1-inch headspace. Next, ladle the leftover liquid from the tomato mixture into each jar, leaving a generous 1-inch headspace. Remove any trapped air pockets and add additional liquid to keep the required headspace.

4 Wipe the rim of each jar with a clean washcloth dipped in vinegar. Place a lid and ring on each jar and hand-tighten.

5 Place the jars in the pressure canner filled with 3 quarts of water, lock the pressure canner lid, and bring the canner to a boil on high heat. Let the canner vent for 10 minutes. Process at 10 psi or according to your canner type and elevation. Process quarts for 20 minutes and pints for 15 minutes.

6 Allow canner to return to zero psi before removing the canner lid. Wait 5 minutes before removing the jars from the canner.

To the Table

Italian Sausage & Peppers

MAKES APPROX. 6 SERVINGS

Use your home canned Basil Diced Tomatoes to create a quick and easy meal in minutes. When you have limited time to get a hearty meal on the table, know this winner will help take the load off. Serve this delicious combination with a small spinach salad and a hot slice of focaccia bread.

3 tablespoon extra-virgin olive oil

6 Italian sausage links, sweet or hot

2 quarts Basil Diced Tomatoes

½ cup red wine

1 tablespoon red pepper flakes

8 fresh basil leaves

1 In a large, 3-inch deep skillet with lid, add the olive oil and sausage links. Using medium-high heat, brown sausage on both sides.

2 Add Basil Diced Tomatoes, wine, and red pepper flakes and stir.

3 Reduce heat to low and cover skillet with lid. Simmer for about 20 minutes or until sausages are cooked through.

4 Using a serving spoon, evenly distribute the basil diced tomato mixture onto the plate and top with a sausage. Garnish with fresh basil leaves and serve hot.

Ingredient Tip

Incorporate more vegetables for a robust one-skillet meal. Add 2 cups of sliced mushrooms, 2 cups diced eggplant, and 1 cup diced zucchini to the skillet when adding the Basil Diced Tomatoes. Not a fan of meat? Feel free to use your favorite meat alternative when making this dish.

Canning Dried Beans  To the Jar

I love having rehydrated, cooked beans on the ready. These are a great addition to soups and stews and make meal creation a breeze, especially for Mexican dishes.

There is no need to pre-soak dried beans when pressure canning. Pressure canning exposes the jar's contents to temperatures upwards of 250°F for up to 90 minutes. This softens and cooks the beans, making them safe for consumption.

Depending on which dried bean you would like to preserve, use the following Dried Bean Chart to know how much of each bean type is required for each jar size.

Dried Ingredient	Quantity per Pint Jar	Quantity per Quart Jar
Black Beans	¾ cup	1 ½ cups
Garbanzo Beans (Chickpeas)	¾ cup	1 ½ cups
Great Northern Beans	½ cup	1 cup
Navy Beans	¾ cup	1 ½ cups
Pinto Beans	½ cup	1 cup
Cannellini Beans	½ cup	1 cup
Kidney Beans	½ cup	1 cup

1 Rinse your dried beans in a colander in the sink. Using both hands, lift and sift the beans ensuring every bean is getting rinsed with the fresh water. Remove and discard any stones and disfigured beans.

2 Place the rinsed beans into a large bowl or pot and cover with water. Remove and discard any beans that float to the surface of the water. Using your hands, mix beans well to clean. Empty the beans back into the colander and rinse again.

3 Using the Dried Bean Chart and a funnel, place the required amount of cleaned dried beans into each jar. Ladle water into each jar filling to a 1-inch headspace. Remove any trapped air pockets and add additional water if necessary to maintain the 1-inch headspace.

4 Wipe the rim of each jar with a clean washcloth dipped in vinegar. Place a lid and ring on each jar and hand-tighten.

5 Place the jars in the pressure canner filled with 3 quarts of cool water, lock the pressure canner lid, and warm the canner on medium heat for 10 minutes. After canner has warmed, bring the canner to a boil on high heat. Let the canner vent for 10 minutes. Process at 10 psi or according to your canner type and elevation. Process quarts for 90 minutes and pints for 75 minutes.

6 Allow canner to return to zero psi before removing the canner lid. Wait 5 minutes before removing the jars from the canner.

Ingredient Tip

Do you have hard water? Not to worry. Create your own soft water by combining 3 tablespoons of salt to every 1 gallon (16 cups) of water for every 1 pound (16 ounces) of dried beans.

Pinto Bean Casserole

MAKES APPROX. 6-8 SERVINGS

This casserole gives your tastebuds a wakeup call with intense flavors and textures. By using pinto beans and meat as the base and cornbread on top, this becomes the perfect dinner solution for hungry families. Be sure to get creative with the toppings, like fresh cut cilantro, a dollop of sour cream, a scoop of guacamole, or a side of your favorite salsa.

1 pound ground beef

1 quart, or 2 pints, pinto beans

1 cup diced sweet onion

1 pint of Basil Diced Tomatoes (page 75)

1 pint whole kernel corn, drained (or 1 ½ cups frozen)

¾ cup tomato paste, store-bought or homemade

2 cups shredded cheddar cheese

1 8.5-ounce Jiffy cornbread mix

1 egg

⅓ cup milk

1 Preheat over to 350°F. Heat a skillet on medium-high and brown the ground beef. Drain any fat.

2 Add pinto beans, onions, tomatoes, and corn to the meat and heat through. Add tomato paste and mix well to evenly coat the ingredients with the paste.

3 Heat a skillet on medium-high and brown the ground beef. Drain any fat. Add pinto beans, onions, tomatoes, and corn to the meat and heat through. Add tomato paste and mix well to evenly coat the ingredients with the paste.

4 Empty contents of skillet into a greased 9x13 baking dish. Sprinkle with cheese covering every part of the pinto meat mixture.

5 In a mixing bowl, combine cornbread mix, egg, and milk. Pour over the pinto bean casserole and evenly spread.

6 Bake uncovered for 30 to 40 minutes or until cornbread is lightly brown and a toothpick comes out clean when inserted into its center. Remove from oven and let sit 10 minutes before serving.

Sausage & Bean Soup

MAKES APPROX. EIGHT 8-OUNCE SERVINGS

This delicious soup is one of my family's favorites. Packed full of protein and fresh vegetables, this hearty soup gives your family a healthy, filling meal in minutes. During the cold, winter months, a bowl of this piping hot soup will warm you from the inside out.

2 tablespoons extra virgin olive oil

4 garlic cloves, minced

1 large onion, finely diced

1 ½ pounds ground Italian sausage

8 cups beef stock

4 carrots, cut into ½-inch round pieces

2 celery stalks, cut into ½-inch pieces

2 bay leaves

1 pint black beans

1 pint pinto beans

1 pint great northern beans

½ teaspoon sea salt

¼ teaspoon black pepper

½ bunch kale leaves, stem and main vein removed, coarsely chopped

1 In a large stockpot combine olive oil, garlic, and onions. Sauté on medium heat until onions are softened, about 5 minutes. Add Italian sausage and cook until done, breaking sausage into smaller, bite-size pieces using a wooden spoon.

2 Add beef stock, carrots, and celery. Increase heat to medium-high and bring to a boil. Add bay leaves and boil for an additional 5 minutes.

3 Next, add the black beans, pinto beans, great northern beans, salt, and pepper to the stockpot and mix well. Return to a boil, then reduce heat and simmer for 10 minutes.

4 Add chopped kale and continue to simmer for an additional 5 minutes, stirring occasionally.

5 Ladle hot soup into bowls. Serve with a hot slice of beer bread or a handful of oyster crackers.

Recipe Tip

If you wanted to create this recipe and preserve it in a jar, you may do so. Fill jars to 1-inch headspace and process at 10 psi or according to your canner type and elevation. Process quarts for 90 minutes and pints for 75 minutes.

Hummus Starter

MAKES APPROX. 3 QUARTS OR 6 PINTS

Hummus has become popular across the globe. It is enjoyed as an appetizer, snack and even a diet food. Save time in the kitchen with this easy hummus starter making homemade hummus in a cinch.

3 cups dried garbanzo beans

3 tablespoons minced garlic

3 teaspoons ground cumin

3 teaspoons salt

1 Rinse your dried garbanzo beans in a colander in the sink. Using both hands, lift and sift the beans ensuring every bean is getting rinsed with the water. Remove and discard any stones and disfigured beans.

2 Using a funnel, add 1 ½ cups of dried garbanzo beans to each quart jar. Next, add to each quart jar 1 tablespoon of minced garlic, 1 teaspoon ground cumin, and 1 teaspoon salt. If canning in pints, add ¾ cup dried garbanzo beans, ½ tablespoon of minced garlic, ½ teaspoon ground cumin, and ½ teaspoon salt.

3 Ladle water into each jar filling to a 1-inch headspace. Remove any trapped air pockets and add additional water if necessary to maintain the 1-inch headspace.

4 Wipe the rim of each jar with a clean washcloth dipped in vinegar. Place a lid and ring on each jar and hand-tighten.

5 Place the jars in the pressure canner filled with 3 quarts of cool water, lock the pressure canner lid, and warm the canner on medium for 10 minutes. After canner has warmed, bring the canner to a boil on high heat. Let the canner vent for 10 minutes. Process at 10 psi or according to your canner type and elevation. Process quarts for 90 minutes and pints for 75 minutes.

6 Allow canner to return to zero psi before removing the canner lid. Wait 5 minutes before removing the jars from the canner.

Recipe Tip

Ready to use? Simply empty a jar into a food processor and follow your favorite hummus recipe. Serve with pita bread or your favorite veggies.

Ultimate Roasted Red Pepper Hummus

To the Table

MAKES APPROX. 6 TO 8 SERVINGS

This authentic hummus has all the faves! Using roasted red bell peppers, tahini paste, a touch of sumac, and a sprinkle of roasted pine nuts, your loved ones will ask for this hummus time and time again. Drizzle with extra-virgin olive oil before serving with warm pita bread and sliced raw carrots and celery.

1 red bell pepper, seeded and cut into strips

3 tablespoons extra-virgin olive oil, divided

1 pint hummus starter (do not drain)

2 garlic cloves

5 tablespoons tahini paste

1 teaspoon sumac

1 teaspoon smoked paprika

2 tablespoons lemon juice

2 tablespoons pine nuts, roasted

Ingredient Tip

If you have home canned roasted peppers in your pantry, this would be an excellent recipe to use them. When doing so, there is no need to add olive oil as the home canned peppers should provide ample oil and moisture.

1 Place red bell pepper strips into cast iron skillet and drizzle with 2 tablespoons of olive oil. Roast on the stovetop or in the oven at 450°F until tender and lightly charred. Remove from heat, let cool, and drain excess oil.

2 Using a food processor, add roasted bell peppers, 1 pint hummus starter including any liquid, garlic cloves, tahini paste, sumac, paprika, and lemon juice. Add remaining tablespoon of olive oil. Turn food processor on high and blend until creamy.

3 Turn off food processor and scrape any foods from the side into the center blade and run the food processor again to ensure a consistent blend.

4 Using a food processor, add roasted bell peppers, 1 pint hummus starter including any liquid, garlic cloves, tahini paste, sumac, paprika, and lemon juice. Add remaining tablespoon of olive oil. Turn food processor on high and blend until the hummus is creamy. Turn off food processor and scrape any foods from the side into the center blade and run the food processor again to ensure a consistent blend.

5 Lightly toast the pine nuts in the same skillet on the stove top for 1 to 2 minutes.

6 Transfer hummus to a serving bowl. roasted pine nuts on top of hummus, cover, and chill in the refrigerator until ready to serve. When ready to serve, remove cover, drizzle extra-virgin olive oil on top, and sprinkle with a pinch of paprika.

Naturally Flavored Applesauce

MAKES 8 TO 10 PINTS OR 4 TO 6 QUARTS

This delicious spin on a traditional favorite gives you and your family a healthy alternative to store-bought applesauce. Enjoy the fun colors the fruits produce in these four easy-to-make options.

Blueberry Applesauce

12 pounds Golden Delicious or Fuji apples, cored, quartered (skins on)
5 cups blueberries
4 cups water
5 tablespoons bottled lemon juice
1-3 cups granulated sugar, to taste

Cinnamon Applesauce

12 pounds Golden Delicious or Fuji apples, cored, quartered (skins on)
3 tablespoons ground cinnamon
4 cups water
5 tablespoons bottled lemon juice
1-3 cups granulated sugar, to taste

Pear Applesauce

12 pounds Golden Delicious or Fuji apples, cored, quartered (skins on)
5 pounds pears, peeled, cored, and sliced
4 cups water
5 tablespoons bottled lemon juice
1-3 cups granulated sugar, to taste

Strawberry Applesauce

12 pounds Golden Delicious or Fuji apples, cored, quartered (skins on)
7 cups strawberries, hulled and halved
4 cups water
5 tablespoons bottled lemon juice
1-3 cups granulated sugar, to taste

1 For each option, in a large stockpot combine quartered apples, fruit or cinnamon, and water. Bring to a boil over medium-high heat. Reduce heat and boil gently while stirring frequently to avoid scorching. Continue boiling for 20 minutes or until the apple mixture is tender. Remove from heat and let cool.

2 Working in batches, transfer apple mixture into a food mill or food processor and purée until smooth. You may also press apple mixture through a chinois.

3 Return purée to a large thick-bottomed saucepan and add lemon juice and sugar. Mix well. Bring to a boil over medium-high heat, stirring frequently to avoid scorching. Boil for 5 minutes then remove from heat.

4 Using a funnel, ladle applesauce into hot jars, leaving a ½-inch of headspace. Remove any air pockets and add additional applesauce if necessary to maintain the ½-inch headspace.

5 Wipe the rim of each jar with a clean washcloth dipped in vinegar. Place a lid and ring on each jar and hand-tighten.

6 Place the jars in the water bather filled with 3 quarts of water, ensuring each jar is covered by at least 1-inch of water. Bring the canner to a boil on high heat and process quarts and pints for 20 minutes. Do not start your timer until the water is at a full rolling boil. After processing, wait 5 minutes before removing the jars from the canner.

Tart Cherry Pie Filling

MAKES APPROX. 5 QUARTS OR 10 PINTS

This gorgeous and delicious pie filling makes wonderful pies, tarts, and toppings. This tart and rich filling is a lovely gift for any occasion!

10 pounds tart cherries, pitted

3 ½ cups raw sugar

1 cup Canning Gel (ClearJel®)

1 teaspoon ground cinnamon

¼ cup lemon juice

Ingredient Tip

If your drained cherries do not yield 4 cups of juice, you may use store-bought Tart Cherry Juice in its place. Especially if you are doubling or tripling the recipe.

1 Place a colander atop a large bowl and add all 10 pounds of cherries. Lightly press cherries into the colander to extrapolate their juice. Cover colander with a dish towel or cheesecloth to keep pests away. Allow cherries to drain for 2 hours or until you have collected roughly 6 to 8 cups of juice. Keep both the cherries and their juice for later.

2 Add 4 cups of cherry juice to a large stainless steel stockpot. Whisk in sugar, Canning Gel, and cinnamon. Bring to a boil over medium-high heat, whisking often to avoid scorching. As the mixture begins to bubble, add the lemon juice. Set timer and boil for 1 minute being sure to whisk constantly. Add all the cherries at once, return to a boil stirring constantly and gently so the cherries are kept intact, about 5 minutes. Remove from heat.

3 Using a funnel, ladle pie filling into hot jars leaving a full 1-inch headspace. Remove air bubbles and add additional filling if necessary to maintain the 1-inch headspace.

4 Wipe the rim of each jar with a clean washcloth dipped in vinegar. Place a lid and ring on each jar and hand-tighten.

5 Place the jars in the water bather filled with 3 quarts of water, ensuring each jar is covered by at least 2-inches of water. Bring the canner to a boil on high heat and process pints and quarts for 35 minutes. Do not start your timer until the water is at a full rolling boil. After processing, wait 5 minutes before removing the jars from the canner.

Mumma Newton's Dough Recipe

My mumma's dough recipe is handwritten on a tattered recipe card tucked away in her stack of cherished family recipes. Used most of her life, this recipe has fed us many times throughout my life. Use this dough recipe to make pie crusts, pasties, Blonde Goddess Sweet Calzones (page 139), and so much more!

2 heaping cups of flour

1 heaping teaspoon sea salt

2 pinches baking powder

1 heaping cup of vegetable shortening (my mumma swears by Butter Flavored Crisco®)

A small, stainless steel bowl of ice water with 3 ice cubes

Ingredient Tip

For pies, divide the dough in half and roll two 10-inch circles with a ¼-inch thickness. Use one as the base of your pie and the other as a cover. Be sure to cut the top for proper ventilation during cooking.

1 In a large bowl, combine flour, salt, and baking powder. Working in batches, hand sift the flour mixture into a clean bowl. Set aside.

2 In a clean large mixing bowl, add 2 tablespoons shortening and 2 tablespoons of the flour mixture. Hand-knead and blend ingredients together. Add an additional 2 tablespoons of shortening and flour mixture plus 2 tablespoons of ice water. Knead together. Continue to add shortening and flour mixture in this pattern, only adding additional water to create a slightly sticky consistency. The dough should be crumbly with bits of shortening throughout. If it becomes too wet or sticky, lightly dust with flour and knead.

3 Once all ingredients are kneaded together, using a rubber spatula, pull every bit of dough from the sides of the bowl to the center. Form dough into a round ball and place back into the bowl. Cover with plastic wrap and place in refrigerator for 1 hour or until ready to use.

Pineapple Chunks in Syrup

MAKES APPROX. 5 PINTS OR 10 HALF-PINTS

Having home canned pineapple on hand is such a treat and a huge cost-savings when pineapple is not in-season. Pineapple has many health benefits and is such a pleasure during the cold, winter months. It is like bringing a bit of the tropics and sunshine into your home when the skies are dark and grey.

2 large pineapples, cored, peeled, and cut into 2-inch chunks (reserve the cores)

6 cups water

½ cup sugar

1 In a deep saucepan with lid, add the two pineapple cores, water, and sugar. Bring to a boil on medium-high heat and stir until sugar dissolves. Let boil for gently for 10 minutes, then remove from heat and cover. Set aside for later.

2 Raw pack your jars with the pineapple chunks, working to fit as many into the jar as possible, filling to ½-inch headspace.

3 Using a funnel, ladle hot syrup over the pineapple chunks filling to a ½-inch headspace. Remove any trapped air pockets and add additional syrup as necessary to maintain the ½-inch headspace.

4 Wipe the rim of each jar with a clean washcloth dipped in vinegar. Place a lid and ring on each jar and hand-tighten.

5 Place the jars in the water bather, ensuring each jar is covered by at least 1-inch of water. Bring the canner to a boil on high heat and process pints and half-pints for 15 minutes. If preserving in quarts, process for 20 minutes. Do not start your timer until the water is at a full rolling boil. After processing, wait 5 minutes before removing the jars from the canner.

To the Table

Hawaiian Sausage Appetizer

SERVES 8 TO 10 PEOPLE

Add a bit of tropical splendor to any get together with this deliciously simple recipe. The combination of home canned sweet pineapple chunks and tangy BBQ sauce gives this dish its fantastic flavor. Wow your guests and your taste buds!

2 tablespoons butter, divided

42 ounces pre-cooked Kielbasa Sausage, cut into 2-inch pieces

6 bratwursts (sweet or spicy), cut into 2-inch pieces

½ cup water

3 pints Pineapple Chunks with Syrup

2 cups BBQ Sauce

Ingredient Tip

Wish to add a bit of crunch to this dish? Cut red and green bell peppers into 2-inch pieces and skewer them in between each piece of pineapple and sausage.

1 In a skillet on medium-high heat, melt 1 tablespoon of butter and add half of the sausage and brown on all sides. Place browned sausage into a crockpot. Add the other tablespoon of butter to the skillet and brown the remaining sausage and place into crockpot.

2 Using the same skillet, add water and bratwursts pieces. Cover skillet with lid and cook for 8 to 10 minutes or until bratwursts are cooked all the way through. Using tongs, add bratwurst pieces to the crockpot.

3 Turn the crockpot on high. Add two pints of Pineapple Chunks with Syrup to the crockpot. Drain the third pint of Pineapple Chunks and add pineapple chunks to the crockpot. Mix well. Add your favorite BBQ sauce and mix to evenly coat meat and pineapple.

4 Heat on high for one hour, mixing a few times to distribute heat. Reduce heat to low and cook for another hour before serving.

Fruit Cocktail

MAKES APPROX.
7 QUARTS, 14 PINTS, OR 28 HALF-PINTS

Say goodbye to store-bought fruit cocktail and hello to your new favorite fruit in the pantry! This mixture is sure to put a smile on everyone's face. The delicious flavor of each fruit works beautifully together and can be preserved in whichever jar size suits your needs. Plus, with the limited amount of sugar and the use of honey, this special treat relies on natural sugar for its sweetness.

½ cup bottled lemon juice with 4 cups water

3 pounds peaches (12 medium), peeled and chopped (9 cups)

2 pounds pears (8 medium), peeled and chopped (4 cups)

4 cups water

2 ½ cups sugar

1 cup honey

2 pounds green seedless grapes (4 cups)

2 12-ounce mangoes, peeled and chopped (2 cups)

1 pound cherries, fresh or frozen, left whole or cut in half (3 cups)

1 pineapple, peeled, cored, and chopped (4 cups)

1 In a non-reactive bowl, mix together the bottled lemon juice and water to create a citric acid bath to prevent your fruit from browning during preparation. As you peel and cut your peaches and pears, place into citric acid bath. Drain in colander before using in the recipe.

2 Place water, sugar, and honey in a large stockpot and bring to a boil over medium-high heat. Stir often to dissolve the sugar.

3 Add the peaches, pears, grapes, chopped mango, cherries, and pineapple chunks to the sugar mixture. Mix well and boil gently for 5 minutes.

4 Using a funnel, ladle fruit into hot jars leaving a 1-inch headspace. Ladle liquid over fruit, filling to ½-inch headspace.

5 Wipe the rim of each jar with a clean washcloth dipped in vinegar. Place a lid and ring on each jar and hand-tighten.

6 Place the jars in the water bather, ensuring each jar is covered by at least 1-inch of water. Bring the canner to a boil on high heat and process quarts for 25 minutes and pints and half-pints for 20 minutes. Do not start your timer until the water is at a full rolling boil. After processing, wait 5 minutes before removing the jars from the canner.

To the Table

Fruit Cocktail Cake

MAKES APPROX. 12 SERVINGS

Simple, moist, flavorful, not overly sweet. This is the best way to describe this amazing cake. Need a dessert in a pinch? Look no further. My daughter and I make this several times a year for planned events, but we love baking this treat when we need a bit of cheer on a snowy day. Give this one a try. You'll thank me.

2 cups all-purpose flour

3 teaspoons baking powder

½ teaspoon salt

1 pint Fruit Cocktail (do not drain)

2 large eggs

1 teaspoon vanilla extract

1 ½ cups granulated sugar

1 Preheat oven to 350°F. Spray a 9x13 baking dish with nonstick cooking spray.

2 In large mixing bowl, combine flour, fruit cocktail, eggs, vanilla extract, and sugar. Using an electric handheld mixer on low speed, thoroughly mix the ingredients. Do not over mix to avoid breaking up the fruit pieces.

3 Pour cake batter into baking dish. Spread evenly with a rubber spatula.

4 Bake at 350°F for 30 to 40 minutes or until lightly browned. A toothpick inserted in the center should come out clean.

Recipe Tip

Wish to add a bit of homemade icing to your cake? Here is a quick recipe you may use right away or store in the refrigerator until ready to use:

½ cup salted butter, softened

4 cups powdered sugar

1 teaspoon vanilla extract

4 tablespoons milk

Add ingredients to a bowl and beat until smooth. Spread atop cake once it has cooled.

Mangoes in Light Syrup

MAKES APPROX. 5 QUARTS, 9 PINTS, OR 18 HALF-PINTS

Sliced mangoes in light syrup are an excellent pantry item for long-term storage. Whether you wish to make smoothies, fruit salads, cocktails, or desserts, this versatile exotic fruit is divine. Don't feel like preserving in slices? No worries! Cut the mango however it fits your needs before packing into jars.

7 cups water

1 cup granulated sugar

27 medium ripe mangoes, peeled and sliced

10 tablespoons bottled lemon juice

1 In a large pot, combine water and sugar. On medium-high heat, bring to a boil, stirring until sugar is dissolved. Add cut mango to stockpot and return to a boil. Boil for 5 minutes then remove from heat.

2 Add the following amount of bottled lemon juice into each hot jar: 2 tablespoons in each quart, 1 tablespoon in each pint or half-pint.

3 Using a slotted spoon, tightly pack each jar with hot mango pieces, leaving a 1-inch headspace.

4 Using a funnel, ladle hot mango syrup into jars, covering mango pieces and filling to ½-inch headspace. Remove any air bubbles and add additional syrup if necessary to maintain the ½-inch headspace.

5 Wipe the rim of each jar with a clean washcloth dipped in vinegar. Place a lid and ring on each jar and hand-tighten.

6 Place the jars in the water bather, ensuring each jar is covered by at least 1-inch of water. Bring the canner to a boil on high heat and process quarts for 20 minutes and pints and half-pints for 15 minutes. Do not start your timer until the water is at a full rolling boil. After processing, wait 5 minutes before removing the jars from the canner.

Simple Mango Ice Cream

MAKES APPROX. 8 SERVINGS

My friend makes simple fruit and frozen cherry ice cream all winter long. She loves thawing her spring picked berries, so I thought, why not use my home canned mangoes to create the same. Easily turn your home canned fruit creations into delicious frozen treats, using this simple recipe!

1 quart Mangoes in Light Syrup, drained

14 ounces sweetened condensed milk, chilled

2 cups cold heavy whipping cream

Ingredient Tip

Feel free to use any of your home canned fruits such as Pineapple Chunks in Syrup (page 95) to make this deliciously simple ice cream.

1 Open a quart jar of Mangoes in Light Syrup and empty into a mesh sieve placed over a bowl. Let drain for 30 minutes.

2 Using a blender, or a stick emulsion blender, purée drained mango pieces in a mixing bowl. Add condensed milk and mix on medium speed until smooth and creamy.

3 In a separate mixing bowl, beat the heavy whipping cream until it forms soft peaks and sticks to the beaters, about 4 to 6 minutes. Using a rubber spatula, fold in mango mixture, stirring gently until smooth.

4 Transfer mixture to freezer-safe container and place in freezer for 8 hours or overnight.

5 When ready to serve, remove from the freezer and let it sit at room temperature for 5 minutes before scooping. Serve immediately or alongside a piece of Fruit Cocktail Cake (page 100).

CHAPTER 4

Salsas & Chutneys

Explore fun recipes and unique ways to incorporate salsa and chutney into your everyday cooking and eating. This chapter gives a variety of canning recipes and fun ways to use your home canned goods to make appetizers, main course dishes, and even desserts.

Tart & Tangy Cherry Salsa

MAKES APPROX. 4 PINTS OR 8 HALF-PINTS

Incorporating cherries in your salsa is an amazing way to bring new life to an otherwise traditional dish. The combination of sweet and heat, and in this case a bit of tart and tangy, really makes cherry salsa unique and incredibly delicious. Whether you simply want to pop open a jar and eat with chips, use it to stuff a pork loin or large chicken breast, or serve it over a brick of softened cream cheese, this salsa is a total crowd pleaser.

3 pounds frozen tart cherries, thawed (8 cups)

1 large red onion, finely chopped (1 ½ cups)

1 cup coarsely chopped fresh cilantro

1 large jalapeño, finely chopped (½ cup)

¼ cup lime juice

4 tablespoons granulated sugar

3 garlic cloves, minced

½ teaspoon salt

1 In a large stockpot, combine cherries, onion, cilantro, jalapeño, lime juice, sugar, garlic, and salt. Bring to a boil over medium-high heat. Reduce heat and simmer for 10 minutes, stirring often.

2 Using a funnel and slotted spoon, fill each jar ¾ full of salsa. Ladle remaining juice over salsa keeping ½-inch headspace. Remove any air bubbles and add more salsa to maintain the ½-inch headspace.

3 Wipe the rim of each jar with a clean washcloth dipped in vinegar. Place a lid and ring on each jar and hand-tighten.

4 Place the jars in the water bather, ensuring each jar is covered by at least 1-inch of water. Bring the canner to a boil on high heat and process pints for 20 minutes and half-pints for 15 minutes. Do not start your timer until the water is at a full rolling boil. After processing, wait 5 minutes before removing the jars from the canner.

Salsa Verde

To the Jar

MAKES APPROX. 3 QUARTS, 6 PINTS, OR 12 HALF-PINTS

Transcend your favorite Mexican dishes by drizzling this amazing salsa over tacos, burritos, tostadas, quesadillas, and refried beans. Use a pint of this flavorful salsa when baking enchilada verdes.

32 tomatillos (6 pounds), husks removed and halved

2 white onions, chopped (3 cups)

2-4 jalapeños, destemmed and finely chopped (1 to 2 cups)

12 garlic cloves, minced (2 tablespoons)

1 cup fresh lime juice

1 tablespoon ground cumin

2 teaspoons smoked paprika

2 teaspoons salt

½ cup coarsely chopped fresh cilantro

Ingredient Tip

If you have green tomatoes to use, feel free to swap out tomatillos for 6 pounds of green tomatoes to create this tart and delicious salsa.

1 Preheat the oven to 450°F. Using a rimmed baking sheet, place tomatillos flesh-side down onto the sheet and roast for 20 minutes or until the tomatillos are lightly charred and soft. Remove from oven and let cool.

2 Using a food processor, purée the onions, jalapeños, and garlic cloves. Empty mixture into a large stockpot. Working in batches, purée the cooled roasted tomatillos and their juice and add to the stockpot. Mix well.

3 Add to the stockpot the lime juice, cumin, paprika, and salt. Mix well and bring to a boil over medium-high heat. Stir often to distribute heat and avoid scorching. Reduce heat and simmer for 15 minutes, stirring occasionally. Add cilantro, mix well, then remove from heat.

4 Using a funnel, ladle the salsa into hot jars leaving a ½-inch of headspace. Remove any air bubbles and add additional salsa if necessary to maintain the ½-inch headspace.

5 Wipe the rim of each jar with a clean washcloth dipped in vinegar. Place a lid and ring on each jar and hand-tighten.

6 Place the jars in the water bather, ensuring each jar is covered by at least 1-inch of water. Bring the canner to a boil on high heat and process quarts for 25 minutes and pints and half-pints for 20 minutes. Do not start your timer until the water is at a full rolling boil. After processing, wait 5 minutes before removing the jars from the canner.

To the Table

Easy Chicken Posole Verde

MAKES APPROX. 6 SERVINGS

Flavors dance in your mouth with my easy chicken posole. Incorporate many of your home canned goods to create this quick, easy, and delicious meal in under 30 minutes. Highlight authentic flavor by using green tomatoes and a jar of your salsa verde. If you don't have access to green tomatoes, no worries! Feel free to use tomatillos instead.

15 medium green tomatoes, cored and chopped (4 cups)

1 orange bell pepper, chopped (1 cup)

1 medium sweet onion, chopped (1 cup)

2 tablespoons minced garlic

1 half-pint Salsa Verde

1 quart chicken stock (4 cups)

1 quart canned chicken breasts (4 cups)

1 pint pinto beans

1 cup frozen corn kernels

1 tablespoon oregano

1 tablespoon ground cumin

2 teaspoons coarse salt

½ cup coarsely chopped fresh cilantro

1 In a large, 3-inch-deep skillet on medium-high heat, cook the green tomatoes, bell pepper, onions, and garlic for 8 minutes or until onions are translucent.

2 Add the home canned salsa verde to the skillet and heat through, about 5 minutes. Add the chicken stock, canned chicken breasts, pinto beans, frozen corn kernels, oregano, ground cumin, and salt. Mix well.

3 Continue to heat through on medium-high heat, working to shred apart the chicken pieces. Cook for an additional 10 minutes then add the fresh cilantro. Mix well and remove from heat.

4 Ladle into bowls and top with additional cilantro. Serve hot.

Ingredient Tip

Feel free to get creative with your toppings. Add a dollop of sour cream or cream cheese. Add chives instead of cilantro or a few dashes of your favorite hot sauce. The possibilities are endless!

Black Bean and Corn Salsa

To the Jar

MAKES APPROX. 6 PINTS

This salsa is delicious on the end of a tortilla chip but is also very versatile. Incorporate this salsa into chili, soups, stews, and even baked goods. I use it when making stuffed bell peppers and baked chicken (mixing a pint with 1 cup of mayo makes a great topping!).

24 medium Roma tomatoes, cored and chopped (8 cups)

2 large red onions, chopped (2 cups)

2 jalapeño peppers, finely chopped (1 cup)

1 green bell pepper (1 cup)

1 cup corn kernels, fresh or frozen

1 ½ cups black beans, home canned or store-bought

¾ cup apple cider vinegar

½ cup fresh lime juice

½ cup coarsely chopped fresh cilantro, loosely packed

8 garlic cloves, minced

1 tablespoon of sea salt

½ teaspoon black pepper

1 In a large stainless steel stockpot, combine tomatoes, red onions, jalapeños, bell pepper, corn, black beans, apple cider vinegar, lime juice, cilantro, garlic, salt, and peppers. Bring to a boil on medium-high heat, stirring often to avoid scorching. Reduce heat and simmer for 30 minutes.

2 Using a funnel, ladle salsa into hot jars being sure to leave a ½-inch headspace. Remove any air bubbles and add additional salsa to maintain the ½-inch headspace.

3 Wipe the rim of each jar with a clean washcloth dipped in vinegar. Place a lid and ring on each jar and hand-tighten.

4 Place the jars in the water bather, ensuring each jar is covered by at least 2-inches of water. Bring the canner to a boil on high heat and process quarts for 25 minutes and pints for 20 minutes. Do not start your timer until the water is at a full rolling boil. After processing, wait 5 minutes before removing the jars from the canner.

Recipe Tip

Use a slotted spoon and fill each pint ¾ full of salsa. Then, ladle the remaining salsa liquid into each jar, keeping the required headspace.

Santa Fe Corn Bread

MAKES APPROX. 6 TO 8 SERVINGS

Talk about an amazing addition to an otherwise traditional cornbread! Adding a pint of your salsa will give the cornbread flavor, texture, color, and moisture. You will never eat plain 'ol cornbread again! The best part, you may create this recipe with any boxed bread mix or incorporate into your family's homemade bread recipe.

2 cups cornmeal

2 teaspoons baking soda

1 teaspoon salt

1 egg

1 pint Black Bean & Corn Salsa, drained

1 tablespoon butter

Recipe Tip

For added flavor, use bacon grease instead of butter! This will add dimension to your cornbread.

1 Preheat oven to 400°F.

2 In a mixing bowl, combine cornmeal, baking soda, and salt and mix together.

3 In a separate bowl, beat the egg and set aside.

4 Add drained salsa and beaten egg to the dry ingredients and fold well, but don't over stir. Set aside.

5 In your cast iron skillet add butter and melt over medium-high heat. Once melted, turn the heat down to medium so the entire base of the skillet can absorb the heat evenly.

6 Add the cornbread mixture to the skillet. Using a heat resistant mitt, grab the skillet handle and give it a couple quick shakes to ensure the batter is spread evenly and not high in the center. Place in oven and bake for 20-25 minutes or until the center proves clear when inserting a toothpick.

7 Remove from oven and rest on baking rack for 20 minutes before cutting and serving.

Cowboy Caviar Salsa

MAKES APPROX. 3 QUARTS OR 7 PINTS

To the Jar

While Cowboy Caviar is best served fresh with avocado, canners across the globe understand the need to have fresh produce preserved for out-of-season months. Use this delicious canning recipe to jump-start this beloved summer salsa. When ready to eat, simply pop open a quart, empty into a bowl, and add one pitted and chopped avocado. Serve with your favorite tortilla chips.

16-24 Roma tomatoes, diced (8 cups)

1 large red onion, diced (1 ½ cups)

1 ½ cups black beans, store-bought or home canned, rinsed and drained

1 ½ cups black eyed peas, store-bought or home canned, rinsed and drained

1 cup whole corn kernels, frozen or fresh

1 bell pepper, diced (1 cup)

2 jalapeño peppers, deseeded and finely chopped, (1 cup)

½ cup coarsely chopped fresh cilantro

1 cup red wine vinegar

¾ cup bottled lime juice

3 tablespoons minced garlic

1 tablespoon granulated sugar

2 teaspoons salt

1 teaspoon pepper

1 In a large stainless steel stockpot, combine tomatoes, onions, black beans, black eyed peas, corn, bell pepper, jalapeño, cilantro, red wine vinegar, lime juice, garlic, sugar, salt, and pepper. Mix well and bring to a boil over medium-high heat. Reduce heat and simmer for 30 minutes, stirring often to blend flavors and avoid scorching.

2 Using a slotted spoon and funnel, fill each jar ¾ full of salsa. Next, ladle remaining salsa liquid into each jar leaving a ½-inch headspace. Remove any air bubbles and add additional salsa if necessary to maintain the ½-inch headspace.

3 Wipe the rim of each jar with a clean washcloth dipped in vinegar. Place a lid and ring on each jar and hand-tighten.

4 Place the jars in the water bather, ensuring each jar is covered by at least 2-inches of water. Bring the canner to a boil on high heat and process quarts for 25 minutes and pints 20 minutes. Do not start your timer until the water is at a full rolling boil. After processing, wait 5 minutes before removing the jars from the canner.

20-Minute Chili Dinner

MAKES APPROX. 4 TO 6 SERVINGS

This hassle-free recipe will have dinner on your table in 20 minutes. Incorporating all the classic chili flavors with a hearty helping of protein, will fill your belly and put a smile on your face.

2 pounds ground beef or turkey

$1/4$ cup chili powder

2 tablespoons ground cumin

1 quart Cowboy Caviar Salsa or Black Bean & Corn Salsa (page 115)

Chili Toppings: sour cream, cheddar cheese, fresh cilantro, tortilla strips, tabasco sauce

1 Brown meat in a skillet on medium-high heat for about 8-10 minutes. Drain the fat and return the cooked meat to your skillet.

2 Add the chili powder and cumin, and mix well. Continue to cook for 2 minutes, then add one quart Cowboy Caviar Salsa or Black Bean & Corn Salsa.

3 Return to a boil, then reduce heat to simmer, and cook for an additional 15 minutes. Stir often to blend flavors.

4 Remove from heat, and ladle into bowls. Sprinkle on your favorite toppings and enjoy.

Recipe Tip

For a deeper flavor profile, use or mix different ground meat such as Italian sausage, ground pork, brisket, and even ground venison. Just be sure the total ratio of meat does not exceed two pounds, unless you are doubling the entire recipe.

Tangy Pepper Salsa

MAKES APPROX. 3 QUARTS, 6 PINTS, OR 12 HALF-PINTS

This amazing salsa hits all the right notes. It embodies the right amount of heat, sweet, and tang, making it the perfect complement to any grilled meat, breakfast or simple tortilla chip. Purée this fine mixture and use it as a dipping sauce for chicken tenders, wings, or even Asian spring rolls!

18 medium Roma tomatoes, diced (6 cups)

8 medium carrots, peeled and grated (3 cups)

6 medium peaches, peeled and diced (2 cups)

1 ½ cups cider vinegar

1 ¼ cups brown sugar

1 orange bell pepper (1 cup)

½ cup onion, finely chopped

1 jalapeño peppers, finely chopped (½ cup)

1 ½ teaspoons sea salt

1 ½ teaspoons fresh ground black pepper

¼ cup cilantro, finely chopped

1 In a large, stainless steel stockpot, combine tomatoes, carrots, peaches, vinegar, brown sugar, orange bell pepper, onion, jalapeño, salt, and pepper. Bring to a boil over medium-high heat, stirring often to avoid scorching. Reduce heat and boil gently until mixture starts to thicken, up to one hour. Stir in cilantro and cook for an additional 15 minutes on low heat.

2 Using a funnel, ladle hot salsa into hot jars leaving a ½-inch headspace. Remove any air bubbles and add additional salsa to maintain the ½-inch headspace.

3 Wipe the rim of each jar with a clean washcloth dipped in vinegar. Place a lid and ring on each jar and hand-tighten.

4 Place the jars in the water bather, ensuring each jar is covered by at least 1-inch of water. Bring the canner to a boil on high heat and process quarts for 25 minutes, pints for 20 minutes, and half-pints for 15 minutes. Do not start your timer until the water is at a full rolling boil. After processing, wait 5 minutes before removing the jars from the canner.

To the
Table

Vegetarian Salsa Burgers

MAKES APPROX. 4 TO 6 SERVINGS

Use fresh veggies and your home canned goods to create this effortless, yet delicious vegetarian meal. Black beans, tangy pepper salsa, and your favorite toppings give this salsa burger a fun, dense flavor.

2 pints black beans (page 79)

1 tablespoon extra-virgin olive oil

½ large onion, finely chopped (1 cup)

1 cup Tangy Pepper Salsa

½ cup breadcrumbs

½ cup feta cheese

2 large eggs

1 Preheat oven to 325°F.

2 Drain black beans and rinse in colander in the sink. Pat dry then spread onto a lined baking sheet. Bake for 15 minutes or until partially dry.

3 In a skillet on medium-high heat, add olive oil and onions. Cook for 5 minutes, then add the salsa. Cook, stirring often, until the mixture begins to thicken, about 8 to 10 minutes. Remove from heat.

4 In a large mixing bowl or food processor, add the black beans, onion-salsa mixture, breadcrumbs, feta cheese, and eggs. Using a fork, or pulsing on low in the food processor, mash until the mixture is thick and chunky.

5 Using your hands, take ⅓ cup of the bean mixture, and form a patty. Continue until all the mixture is used.

6 Increase the oven temperature to 375°F. Place patties on a cookie sheet lined with parchment paper. Bake for 10 minutes on each side.

7 Assemble your burger with your favorite toppings and enjoy.

Zesty Tomato Salsa

To the Jar

MAKES APPROX. 4 QUARTS, 8 PINTS, OR 16 HALF-PINTS

By replacing jalapeños with poblano peppers and apple cider vinegar with red wine vinegar, the flavors dance in your mouth. The key flavor and deep red color is derived from the rehydrated chili pepper purée.

9-12 dried California Chili Peppers, destem and deseed

4 cups boiling water

36 medium Roma tomatoes, finely chopped (12 cups)

2 large red onions, finely chopped (3 cups)

3 large Poblano peppers, cored and finely chopped, (3 cups)

1 ½ cups cilantro, finely chopped

15 garlic cloves, minced

¾ cup red wine vinegar

1 tablespoon sea salt

¾ teaspoon red pepper flakes

1 Place your dried chili peppers in a small stainless steel stockpot or mixing bowl. Fully submerge with boiling hot water for 20 minutes to rehydrate. Use a salad plate or bowl on top of the peppers to keep them submerged.

2 In a large, stainless steel stockpot, combine tomatoes, red onion, poblano peppers, cilantro, garlic, vinegar, salt, and red pepper flakes and mix well. Bring to a boil over medium-high heat, stirring often to avoid scorching reduce heat and simmer for 10 minutes.

3 Place the rehydrated chilies in your food processor with a ¼ cup of the chili water. Purée the chili peppers and water until a paste is created. Add paste to the stockpot and mix well, continuing to simmer for an additional 5 minutes.

4 Using a funnel, ladle salsa into hot jars, leaving a ½-inch of headspace. Remove any air bubbles and add additional salsa if necessary to maintain ½-inch headspace.

5 Wipe the rim of each jar with a clean washcloth dipped in vinegar. Place a lid and ring on each jar and hand-tighten.

6 Place the jars in the water bather, ensuring each jar is covered by at least 1-inch of water. Bring the canner to a boil on high heat and process quarts for 20 minutes, pints and half-pints for 15 minutes. Do not start your timer until the water is at a full rolling boil. After processing, wait 5 minutes before removing the jars from the canner.

Rhubarb Apple Chutney

MAKES APPROX. 5 PINTS OR 10 HALF-PINTS

This gorgeous chutney has a tart yet sweet flavor and warm tones, making it perfect for scones, crepes, and pastry fillings. It is also delicious alongside pork as well as any cheese or fruit tray.

10 medium apples, peeled, cored, and chopped (5 cups)

8 large rhubarb ribs, chopped (4 cups)

4 cups granulated sugar

1 cup dried cranberries, packed

Zest of 1 lemon

2 tablespoons lemon juice

1 teaspoon ground cinnamon

1 teaspoon ground nutmeg

Ingredient Tip

Give this spring time rhubarb chutney a deeper fall flavor by adding ½ teaspoon of ground cloves and ½ teaspoon of allspice.

1 In a large, stainless steel stockpot, combine apples, rhubarb, and sugar. On medium heat, bring to a boil. Reduce heat and simmer for 15 minutes, stirring frequently. Add cranberries, lemon zest and juice, cinnamon, and nutmeg. Continue to boil gently for 15 minutes allowing the chutney to thicken.

2 Using a funnel, ladle hot chutney into hot jars leaving a ½-inch of headspace. Remove any air bubbles and add additional chutney if necessary to maintain the ½-inch headspace.

3 Wipe the rim of each jar with a clean washcloth dipped in vinegar. Place a lid and ring on each jar and hand-tighten.

4 Place the jars in the water bather, ensuring each jar is covered by at least 1-inch of water. Bring the canner to a boil on high heat and process pints and half-pints for 15 minutes. Do not start your timer until the water is at a full rolling boil. After processing, wait 5 minutes before removing the jars from the canner.

Pear & Rhubarb Tarte Tatin

APPROX. 4 TO 6 SERVINGS

Give depth and texture to your tarte tatin with Rhubarb Apple Chutney. Complemented with warm undertones of cinnamon and allspice, this scrumptious dessert is sure to please. Serve warm – and if handy, add a small scoop of vanilla ice cream atop each plated piece.

2 large Bartlett pears, peeled

2 rhubarb ribs, ends removed

3 tablespoons butter

1 half-pint jar Rhubarb Apple Chutney

Mumma Newton's Pie Dough (page 92) – or refrigerated store-bought dough

1 Preheat oven to 350°F.

2 Slice each pear into four even lengthwise pieces, cutting straight through the core. Using a paring knife, remove the core and seeds from the two center slices and discard. Cut the rhubarb into 2 ½-inch slices. Wider stalks may be cut in half then cut to length.

3 In a 10-inch oven-safe skillet, melt butter on medium heat, being sure to coat the entire base of the skillet. Arrange the pears and rhubarb in an alternating, circular sequence covering the entire bottom. The design you make in the skillet will represent the top of the tarte tatin.

4 Reduce heat to low and cook for 10 minutes. Using a tablespoon, fill in the gaps surrounding the rhubarb and pears with the chutney. Be sure to use the entire half-pint. Cook for an additional 3 minutes.

5 Place the pie dough atop of the fruit-chutney design, lightly tucking each edge into the sides of the skillet. Place skillet in oven and bake for 30-40 minutes or until the pie dough is a golden brown.

6 Remove from the oven and rest on the stove top. Wearing heat-proof mitts, place a large plate or round platter over top the skillet. Be sure the plate diameter is larger than the skillet. With the palm of your hand firmly pressed in the center of the plate, lift the skillet by its handle with your other hand. In one fluid motion, lift up and flip the skillet onto the plate. Wait for a couple seconds before removing the skillet to ensure the entire tart released from the skillet and is now resting on the plate.

Savory Cherry Chutney

MAKES APPROX. 12 HALF-PINT OR 6 PINT JARS

Use this delicious chutney on any cheese and meat tray to wow your guests with its amazing array of flavors. Its rich flavor complements any meal beautifully, especially alongside poultry. Feel free to use frozen or fresh cherries for this recipe. You may also create this dish with tart cherries to change the chutney's flavor profile and uses.

1 large sweet onion, cut in half and thinly sliced (1 ½ cups)

2 tablespoons agave sweetener

4 pounds sweet cherries, pitted and coarsely chopped (12 cups)

2 large baking apples, peeled, cored, and chopped fine

1 ½ cups raisins

1 cup apple cider vinegar

½ cup sugar

4 garlic cloves, peeled and finely chopped

1 tablespoon mustard seeds

½ teaspoon salt

¼ teaspoon black pepper

1 teaspoon ground allspice

1 In a stockpot on low heat, gently sauté the sliced onions in the agave sweetener until caramelized, about 7-10 minutes. Lightly dust with black pepper, stir, and set aside.

2 To the stockpot, add the cherries, apples, raisins, apple cider vinegar, sugar, garlic, mustard seeds, salt, pepper, and allspice. Bring to a boil over medium-high heat and gently cook for 5 minutes. Stir often to avoid scorching.

3 Using a funnel, ladle chutney into hot jars leaving a ½-inch of headspace. Remove any air bubbles and add additional chutney if necessary to maintain the ½-inch headspace.

4 Wipe the rim of each jar with a clean washcloth dipped in vinegar. Place a lid and ring on each jar and hand-tighten.

5 Place the jars in the water bather, ensuring each jar is covered by at least 1-inch of water. Bring the canner to a boil on high heat and process pints for 15 minutes and half-pints for 10 minutes. Do not start your timer until the water is at a full rolling boil. After processing, wait 5 minutes before removing the jars from the canner.

Stuffed Chicken Breasts

To the Table

MAKES APPROX. 4 SERVINGS

Serving chicken for dinner is a norm in many households – and although healthy, it can get mundane quickly. Change things up by stuffing each breast with home canned Savory Cherry Chutney. Sprinkle with a bit of fresh Parmesan cheese and enjoy!

2 tablespoons extra-virgin olive oil

4 boneless, skinless chicken breasts

1 pint Savory Cherry Chutney

¾ cup shredded Parmesan cheese, divided

1 Preheat oven to 375°F.

2 In a large skillet on medium-high heat, add oil and chicken breasts. Brown both sides of the breast fully, about 4 minutes on each side. Remove from heat and set aside to cool.

3 In a small bowl, mix chutney and ½ cup Parmesan cheese. When breasts are cool to touch, slit a long pocket on the side of the breast, about ¾ of the way in. Do not cut all the way through the breast; the goal is to make a pocket for the chutney mixture to rest inside.

4 Using a tablespoon, fill each chicken breast with at least 3-5 tablespoons of the chutney mixture. Seal each pocket closed with toothpicks. Place the stuffed breasts in an ungreased glass baking dish and cover with foil.

5 Bake for 30 minutes or until juice runs clear from breasts. Remove toothpicks, sprinkle with remaining Parmesan cheese and serve hot with your favorite side dish.

Blonde Curry Apple Chutney

MAKES APPROX. 8 PINT JARS OR 16 HALF-PINTS

I am proud of my signature chutney recipe which embodies vibrant flavors, beautiful color, and gorgeous texture. Use it to brighten up rice, couscous, or steamed vegetables. Or, serve it over baked brie cheese or on a charcuterie board for a boost of flavor.

4 cups white vinegar

2 pounds Golden Delicious or Spartan apples, peeled, cored, and chopped (8 cups)

5 ½ cups golden raisins

4 cups granulated sugar

2 medium onions, chopped (1 cup)

1 red bell pepper, chopped (1 cup)

2 jalapeño peppers, chopped (1 cup)

3 garlic cloves, finely chopped

3 teaspoons yellow curry powder

3 tablespoons mustard seeds

2 tablespoons ground ginger

2 teaspoons ground allspice

2 teaspoons sea salt

1 In a large, stainless steel stockpot, add white vinegar. As you are prepping your apples, place them in the vinegar, giving them a quick stir so the vinegar coats every apple slice to prevent browning.

2 Add golden raisins, sugar, onions, red bell pepper, jalapeño, and garlic. Bring to a boil over medium-high heat. Reduce heat and gently boil for 30 minutes, stirring frequently to avoid scorching.

3 Add yellow curry, mustard seeds, ground ginger, allspice, and salt. Boil gently for 15 minutes, stirring frequently. The mixture should be thick enough to mound on a spoon.

4 Using a funnel, ladle chutney into hot jars leaving a ½-inch headspace. Remove any air bubbles and add additional chutney if necessary to maintain the ½-inch headspace.

5 Wipe the rim of each jar with a clean washcloth dipped in vinegar. Place a lid and ring on each jar and hand-tighten.

6 Place the jars in the water bather, ensuring each jar is covered by at least 1-inch of water. Bring the canner to a boil on high heat and process pints and half-pints for 15 minutes. Do not start your timer until the water is at a full rolling boil. After processing, wait 5 minutes before removing the jars from the canner.

Blonde Goddess Sweet Calzones

To the Table

MAKES APPROX. 8 SERVINGS

Include the kiddos when making this fun appetizer. We often consider this to be a healthy dessert too! You can use refrigerated store-bought pie dough, pop open a jar of Blonde Curry Apple Chutney, and let little hands enjoy scooping and filling their "mini pies."

1 half-pint Blonde Curry Apple Chutney

8 ounces of Brie cheese, cut into 8 equal pieces

15 ounces of pastry dough (either store-bought or Mumma Newton's page 92)

1 egg beaten

1 teaspoon water

1 teaspoon ground cinnamon

1 apple, cored and sliced

1 Preheat oven to 350°F.

2 In a small bowl, gently beat the egg and water together. Set aside.

3 Roll your dough on a lightly floured surface until ¼-inch thick. Cut out eight 6-inch circles.

4 Taking one of the circles of dough, place 2-3 tablespoons of chutney in the center. Add a piece of brie on top.

5 Using a pastry brush, lightly coat the edge of the dough with the egg mixture. Lift the edges of the dough together and pinch together to seal it closed. Lightly brush top of mini pie with egg and dust with ground cinnamon.

6 Place mini pies on a non-stick cookie sheet, or a parchment paper lined baking sheet, and bake for 15-20 minutes, or until the pastry dough is golden brown. It is normal for some cheese and chutney to ooze out.

7 Remove from oven and allow to sit for 3 minutes before serving. Garnish with two apple slices, a slice of Brie, and raisins. Serve warm.

Blonde Chutney Stuffed Pork Loin

The delicious blend of curry and allspice gives pork a delectable flavor and enhances its juiciness. A dish sure to impress, its simplicity makes it easy to serve for any occasion.

1 pint Blonde Curry Apple Chutney

1 ½ pound pork loin, butterflied

Black pepper and sea salt

6" boning knife

Meat mallet

Butchers twine

1 Preheat oven at 375°F.

2 On a large cutting board, starting at the right side of the loin, insert your knife ½-inch thickness from the edge, and cut lengthwise. The goal is to work your way around the exterior of the loin, turning the pork loin one rotation to continue to open the loin. Be sure not to cut all the way through the entire pork loin. On the final rotation, continue to work the knife gently lengthwise until the loin is cut flat. The outcome is to butterfly, or open the loin, creating a flat surface to lay the chutney.

3 Using a meat mallet, pound the loin until it is about ¼- to ½-inch thick. Be careful not to over pound any particular area, doing so will cause holes and tears in the muscle.

4 Spread the chutney atop the loin keeping a 1-inch border from the edge. Starting on the short side, roll the loin pulling and tucking the chutney and meat inward. Any chutney that escapes, simply add into the next roll or slather onto the outside of the loin.

5 Using butchers twine, tie the center of the roll tightly to keep it intact. Next, tie each end then tie any additional areas which may require securing. Dash the stuffed loin with salt and pepper and place into a baking dish.

6 Roast for 1 hour or until internal temperature reaches 150°F and juices run clear. Remove from the oven and rest for 10 minutes before removing twine and cutting. Serve alongside a fresh spinach salad and creamed sweet potatoes.

Gingered Plum Chutney

To the Jar

MAKES APPROX. 7 PINTS OR 14 HALF-PINTS

This chutney is an excellent accompaniment to any meat or poultry dish. One option is to panfry a chicken, add a pint of gingered plum chutney, and serve over a bed of wild rice. It is also delicious served warm over chocolate ice cream.

20 medium plums, pitted and chopped (10 cups)

2 cups dark brown sugar

2 cups apple cider vinegar

2 cups raisins

1 large sweet onion, chopped (1 ½ cups)

1 ounce crystallized ginger, finely chopped

1 tablespoon fresh ginger, finely chopped

1 In a large stockpot, combine the plums, dark brown sugar, vinegar, raisins, onion, crystallized ginger, and fresh ginger. Mix well. Bring to a boil over medium-high heat, stirring often. Reduce heat to low and simmer for 30 minutes, stirring often to avoid scorching.

2 Using a funnel, ladle chutney into hot jars, leaving a ½-inch headspace. Remove any air bubbles and add additional chutney if necessary to maintain the ½-inch headspace.

3 Wipe the rim of each jar with a clean washcloth dipped in vinegar. Place a lid and ring on each jar and hand-tighten.

4 Place the jars in the water bather, ensuring each jar is covered by at least 1-inch of water. Bring the canner to a boil on high heat and process pints and half-pints for 10 minutes. Do not start your timer until the water is at a full rolling boil. After processing, wait 5 minutes before removing the jars from the canner.

Ingredient Tip

Feel free to crystallize your own ginger using a dehydrator. Simply peel and cut 5 to 8 gingerroots into long strips about ⅛- to ¼-inch thick. Then, prepare two fresh vanilla bean pods by slicing them length wise and scraping out the seeds. In a Dutch oven, add ginger slices, 1 tablespoon lemon juice, and vanilla beans and seeds. Gently boil for 30 minutes. Drain, remove vanilla beans, coat all sides of ginger with granulated sugar, and dehydrate at 150° for 4-5 hours or until tender and chewy. Store in an air-tight container for up to 3 months.

Vegetable Chutney

MAKES APPROX. 7 PINTS OR 14 HALF-PINTS

Popular in the United Kingdom, vegetable chutney is the perfect way to enjoy end of the garden vegetables throughout the colder months. This chutney is sweet with just a touch of heat and tartness from the apple cider vinegar. We love this spread on a warm hamburger between a brioche bun. Or, mix a couple tablespoons into traditional hummus for a quick appetizer.

2 pounds apples, peeled, cored and finely chopped (8 cups)

½ pound carrots, shredded (1 ½ cups)

1 small cauliflower head, cut into small florets (2 cups)

2 cups dried apricots, chopped

2 medium onions, finely chopped (1 cup)

1 medium beet, peeled and finely chopped (½ cup)

1 jalapeño, finely chopped (½ cup)

1 ½ cups apple cider vinegar

1 cup light brown sugar

½ cup water

5 garlic cloves, coarsely chopped

3 tablespoons bottled lemon juice

1 tablespoon mustard seeds

2 teaspoons ground allspice

1 In a thick bottomed saucepan or stockpot, combine apples, carrots, cauliflower, dried apricots, onions, beet, jalapeño, apple cider vinegar, brown sugar, water, garlic, lemon juice, mustard seeds, and allspice. Mix well. Over medium-high heat, bring mixture to a boil. Reduce heat and gently boil for 45 minutes, stirring often to avoid scorching.

2 Using a funnel, ladle the chutney into hot jars leaving a ½-inch of headspace. Remove any air bubbles and add additional chutney if necessary to maintain the ½-inch headspace.

3 Wipe the rim of each jar with a clean washcloth dipped in vinegar. Place a lid and ring on each jar and hand-tighten.

4 Place the jars in the water bather, ensuring each jar is covered by at least 1-inch of water. Bring the canner to a boil on high heat and process pints and half-pints for 20 minutes. Do not start your timer until the water is at a full rolling boil. After processing, wait 5 minutes before removing the jars from the canner.

CHAPTER 5

Pickling

The art of pickling is truly simple and fun because you can just about "pickle" anything! Following the given brine ratio of salt, vinegar, and additional liquid, you may pickle any vegetable all year round. This chapter gives you a variety of tasty and simple pickling recipes, ending with a delicious Bloody Mary Mix canning recipe so you may display and enjoy all of your pickled treats.

Dilled Carrot Sticks

MAKES APPROX. 8 PINTS OR 16 HALF-PINTS

Who says pickles need to be green? Enjoy these fresh out of the jar as a quick, healthy snack or on any relish tray. Feel free to alter the amount of red pepper flakes to your liking.

6 cups white vinegar

2 cups water

½ cup pickling and canning salt

8 cloves of garlic

8 heads of dill or 4 teaspoons of dill seeds

4 teaspoons red pepper flakes

8 pounds carrots, peeled and cut into 3 ½ -inch sticks

1 Brine: In a large, stainless steel stockpot, combine vinegar, water, and salt. Bring to a boil over medium-high heat, stirring to dissolve the salt. Boil for 5 minutes then remove from heat.

2 In each pint jar, place one garlic clove, 1 head of dill or ½ teaspoon of dill seeds, and a ½ teaspoon of red pepper flakes, if using. Tightly raw pack the carrots sticks into each jar leaving a ½-inch headspace.

3 Using a funnel, ladle hot brine into warm jars being sure to maintain the ½-inch headspace. Gently tap each jar onto a cutting board to release trapped air pockets. Add additional brine if necessary to maintain the ½-inch headspace.

4 Wipe the rim of each jar with a clean washcloth dipped in vinegar. Place a lid and ring on each jar and hand-tighten.

5 Place the jars in the water bather, ensuring each jar is covered by at least 1-inch of water. Bring the canner to a boil on high heat and process pints and half-pints for 10 minutes. Do not start your timer until the water is at a full rolling boil. After processing, wait 5 minutes before removing the jars from the canner.

Pickled Ramps

MAKES APPROX. 6 HALF-PINTS

The ramp, also called a wild leek, is a wild onion native to North America and is often found when foraging wooded areas. The bulb resembles a scallion and the leaves are broad, flat, and a beautiful deep green. Ramps can be pickled or used fresh in soups in place of onions and garlic.

3 pounds of ramps

3 ¾ cups white vinegar

3 cups water

3 tablespoons pickling and canning salt

6 tablespoons honey

Seasonings Per Jar

¼ teaspoon mustard seeds

¼ teaspoon whole coriander seeds

2-3 whole black peppercorns

1 dried bay leaf

1 Thoroughly wash the ramps. Cut the bulb just above the white, allowing some burgundy stem to remain, which is also known as the taproot.

2 In a large, stainless steel stockpot, combine vinegar, water, salt, and honey to create the brine. Bring to a boil over medium-high heat, stirring to dissolve the salt. Boil for 5 minutes then remove from heat.

3 In each half-pint jar, add ¼ teaspoon mustard seeds, ¼ teaspoon whole coriander seeds, 2-3 whole black peppercorns, and 1 dried bay leaf. Then, raw pack the ramps tightly leaving a ½-inch of headspace.

4 Using a funnel, ladle hot brine into jars being sure to maintain a ½-inch headspace. Gently tap each jar onto a cutting board to release trapped air pockets. Add additional brine if necessary to maintain the ½-inch headspace.

5 Wipe the rim of each jar with a clean washcloth dipped in vinegar. Place a lid and ring on each jar and hand-tighten.

6 Place the jars in the water bather, ensuring each jar is covered by at least 1-inch of water. Bring the canner to a boil on high heat and process half-pints for 15 minutes. Do not start your timer until the water is at a full rolling boil. After processing, wait 5 minutes before removing the jars from the canner.

Ingredient Tip

Keep the green leaves from your ramps! These are great chopped fresh or dehydrated for use in soups and sauces.

Pickled Ramp Martini

MAKES 1 COCKTAIL

For those of you who love plucking a pearl onion in your martini, this recipe is for you! The amazing blend of coriander and garlic coupled with a hint of honey from the brine make an otherwise boring martini new and exciting. Its earthy but sweet flavor will make this your new favorite drink.

2 ½ ounces your favorite vodka

1 half-pint Pickled Ramps

¼ ounce Pickled Ramp juice, less or more, depending on your preference

½ ounce vermouth

Fresh cracked black pepper

1 Place one or two pickled ramps in a chilled martini glass.

2 Fill a martini shaker with ice. Add vodka, your preferred amount of ramp juice (dirty to your liking), and vermouth.

3 Shake very well, up to 45 shakes. The longer the better since you cannot over shake this cocktail.

4 Drain into the martini glass atop the pickled ramp.

5 Crack two turns of fresh black pepper overtop the cocktail and serve.

Pickled Asparagus Spears

To the Jar

MAKES APPROX. 3 QUARTS OR 6 PINTS

The perfect pickled treat for any occasion. Have fun munching on these crunchy spears alongside a frothy beer or a freshly made sandwich and chips. Add the spices to your liking, whether you prefer it hot and spicy or classic garlic and dill.

5 cups white vinegar

5 cups water

½ cup pickling and canning salt

6 cloves of garlic, peeled whole

3 teaspoons dill seeds or 6 fresh dill flower heads

3 teaspoons mustard seed

3 teaspoons red pepper flakes (optional)

11 pounds asparagus

1 Brine: In a large, stainless steel stockpot, combine vinegar, water, and salt. Bring to a boil over medium-high heat, stirring to dissolve the salt. Boil for 5 minutes then remove from heat.

2 In each quart jar, add two garlic cloves, 1 teaspoon dill seeds (or 2 fresh dill flower heads), ½ teaspoon mustard seeds and 1 teaspoon of hot pepper flakes.

3 Remove tough ends from asparagus and trim to fit the height of the jar with 1-inch of head space. Tightly raw pack the asparagus spears into each jar.

4 Using a funnel, ladle hot brine into jars leaving a ½-inch headspace. Gently tap each jar onto a cutting board to release trapped air pockets. Add additional brine if necessary to maintain the ½-inch headspace.

5 Wipe the rim of each jar with a clean washcloth dipped in vinegar. Place a lid and ring on each jar and hand-tighten.

6 Place the jars in the water bather, ensuring each jar is covered by at least 1-inch of water. Bring the canner to a boil on high heat and process quarts for 15 minutes and pints for 10 minutes. Do not start your timer until the water is at a full rolling boil. After processing, wait 5 minutes before removing the jars from the canner.

Ingredient Tip

If wishing to preserve asparagus spears in pint jars, be sure to cut the spear to the height of the pint jar less one inch. For seasonings, add 1 garlic clove, ½ teaspoon dill seeds (or 1 dill flower head), ½ teaspoon mustard seeds, and ½ teaspoon red pepper flakes, (if using) to each pint jar.

Pickled Brussels Sprouts

MAKES APPROX. 6 PINTS

Keep 'em dilled or add a bit of heat using hot pepper flakes. Serving a relish tray for the holidays? Add these round beauties to impress your guests or eat them straight out of the jar! Their size and shape are fun for snacking.

6 cups white vinegar

2 cups water

½ cup pickling and canning salt

3 cloves of garlic, cut in half

12 heads of fresh dill or 3 teaspoons of dill seeds

3 teaspoons hot pepper flakes per jar (optional – I like to make half the jars spicy and the other regular)

4 pounds Brussels sprouts

1 Brine: In a large, stainless steel stockpot, combine vinegar, water, and salt. Bring to a boil over medium-high heat, stirring to dissolve the salt. Boil for 5 minutes then remove from heat.

2 Cut ends of Brussels sprouts, remove outer layer of leaves, and rinse. In each jar, add the following: half a garlic clove, 2 heads of dill or ½ teaspoon of dill seeds, and a ½ teaspoon of hot pepper flakes. Tightly raw pack the Brussels sprouts into each jar leaving a ¾-inch headspace.

3 Using a funnel, ladle hot brine into jars leaving a ½-inch headspace. Gently tap each jar onto a cutting board to release trapped air pockets. Add additional brine if necessary to maintain the ½-inch headspace.

4 Wipe the rim of each jar with a clean washcloth dipped in vinegar. Place a lid and ring on each jar and hand-tighten.

5 Place the jars in the water bather, ensuring each jar is covered by at least 1-inch of water. Bring the canner to a boil on high heat and process pints for 10 minutes. Do not start your timer until the water is at a full rolling boil. After processing, wait 5 minutes before removing the jars from the canner.

Sweet & Spicy Pickled Radishes

To the Jar

MAKES APPROX. 6 HALF-PINT JARS

A complimentary mixture of sweet, heat and pepper, these flavors come alive in this pickled recipe making the perfect condiment for sandwiches and salads. There are many varieties of radishes grown across the globe so have fun exploring. And, the deeper the color, the prettier they are in a jar.

1 ½ cups water

1 ¼ cups white vinegar

¼ cup red wine vinegar

¾ cup granulated sugar

1 tablespoon mustard seeds

2 teaspoons pickling and canning salt

2 teaspoons mixed peppercorns

1 teaspoon dried red pepper flakes

2 pounds radishes, tops and roots removed and sliced ⅛-inch thick

1 In a medium saucepan combine water, white vinegar, red wine vinegar, sugar, salt, mustard seeds, peppercorns, and red pepper flakes. On medium-high heat, bring to a boil, stirring until sugar and salt are dissolved. Boil for 10 minutes to infuse flavors then remove from heat.

2 Pack radish slices into hot half-pint jars, leaving a ½-inch of headspace. Using a funnel, ladle hot vinegar mixture into jars being sure to keep the ½-inch headspace. Evenly distribute the peppercorns, seeds, and flakes amongst each jar.

3 Wipe each jar rim with a clean washcloth dipped in vinegar. Add lids and rings and hand tighten.

4 Place the jars in the water bather, ensuring each jar is covered by at least 1-inch of water. Bring the canner to a boil on high heat and process half-pints for 10 minutes. Do not start your timer until the water is at a full rolling boil. After processing, wait 5 minutes before removing the jars from the canner.

Spiced Red Cabbage

MAKES APPROX. 4 QUARTS OR 8 PINTS

Fuchsia in color and robust in flavor, add this side dish to any meal. Spicy red cabbage is perfect for serving warm around the holidays alongside ham or pork. I will often mix one quart of spiced cabbage with a half-pint of jalapeño jelly, bake it covered at 350°F for 20 minutes and serve. This makes a scrumptious dish with both salty and sweet flavors.

3 medium red cabbages, shredded fine (12 cups)

½ cup pickling and canning salt

2 tablespoons pickling spice

4 cups apple cider vinegar

1 ½ cups granulated sugar

4 cinnamon sticks, broken

Cheesecloth and butcher's twine

1 Quarter the cabbages, remove core, and shred fine. In a large plastic bowl, layer all the cabbage and salt in an alternating fashion. Mix well and cover. Let sit in a refrigerator for 12 hours.

2 Thoroughly rinse the cabbage, making sure all the salt is removed.

Drain in a colander. Raw pack shredded cabbage into pint jars leaving ½-inch of headspace.

3 Place pickling spice in cheesecloth and tie with butchers' twine to create a spice bag. In a stockpot, add vinegar, sugar, cinnamon sticks, and the spice bag. Bring to a boil over medium heat. Stir until sugar is dissolved, then boil for 10 minutes to infuse the flavors. Remove from heat and take out the cinnamon sticks and spice bag and discard.

4 Using a funnel, ladle hot brine into jars, pressing down onto the cabbage to release trapped air pockets. Fill to a ½-inch of headspace.

5 Wipe the rim of each jar with a clean washcloth dipped in vinegar. Place a lid and ring on each jar and hand-tighten.

6 Place the jars in the water bather, ensuring each jar is covered by at least 1-inch of water. Bring the canner to a boil on high heat and process quarts for 30 minutes and pints and half-pints for 20 minutes. Do not start your timer until the water is at a full rolling boil. After processing, wait 5 minutes before removing the jars from the canner.

Pickled Garlic Cloves

To the Jar

MAKES APPROX. 6 HALF-PINTS

Add these beauties to pasta whole or simply mash the cloves to create a paste to spread over a baguette, then top with calamata olives and brie cheese. I opened a jar for a small party at my home, went into the kitchen to grab a serving bowl only to come back to an empty jar. Guests were skewering them straight out of the jar and finished them off before I made it back to the credenza!

2 ½ cups white vinegar

1 cup Pinot Grigio wine

1 tablespoon pickling and canning salt

1 tablespoon sugar

2 tablespoons dried oregano, divided

12-15 large garlic heads, separated and peeled

5-6 dried California Dried Chilies, stems removed

1 Brine: In a large stainless steel stockpot, combine vinegar, wine, salt, sugar, and 1 ½ tablespoons dried oregano. Bring to a boil over medium-high heat, stirring to dissolve the salt. Boil for 5 minutes then remove from heat. Add peeled garlic cloves and cook for and additional minute.

2 Add to each hot jar a pinch of oregano and 1 dried chili pepper. Feel free to cut a pepper in half as they can be long.

3 Using a slotted spoon and funnel, fill each jar with garlic cloves, leaving a ¾ inch headspace. Using a ladle, fill each jar with brine to a ½-inch headspace. Gently tap each jar onto a cutting board to release trapped air pockets. Add additional brine if necessary to maintain the ½-inch headspace.

4 Wipe the rim of each jar with a clean washcloth dipped in vinegar. Place a lid and ring on each jar and hand-tighten.

5 Place the jars in the water bather, ensuring each jar is covered by at least 1-inch of water. Bring the canner to a boil on high heat and process pints and half-pints for 10 minutes. Do not start your timer until the water is at a full rolling boil. After processing, wait 5 minutes before removing the jars from the canner.

Lime Poblano Peppers

MAKES APPROX. 6 PINTS OR 12 HALF-PINTS

This unique blend of flavors makes for the perfect pickled addition to any dish! Spice up your nachos or blend with a fresh jalapeño and a brick of cream cheese for an amazing dip. I will often dice up a few pickled peppers and onions to sprinkle over my chili dogs.

8 poblano peppers, destemmed and sliced into ¼-inch rounds

1 cup thinly sliced sweet onions

4 cups white vinegar

1 cup sweet white wine (Riesling or Moscato)

½ cup water

½ cup bottled lime juice

¼ cup pickling and canning salt

2 tablespoons granulated sugar

2 large limes, cut into 12 slices

6 garlic cloves, minced

1 Cut and prep the poblano peppers and sweet onions and place in a large bowl. Mix together to evenly distribute the onions amongst the peppers. Set aside.

2 In a stainless steel stockpot, combine vinegar, white wine, water, lime juice, salt, and sugar. Bring to a boil over medium-high heat and stir until salt and sugar are dissolved. Boil for 5 minutes, then remove from heat.

3 Add to each pint jar 2 lime slices and 1 teaspoon of minced garlic. If using half-pints, add 1 lime slice and ½ teaspoon of minced garlic to each jar.

4 Tightly raw pack the jars with the pepper onion mixture leaving a ½-inch of headspace. Using a funnel, ladle hot brine into each jar, being sure to keep a ½-inch headspace. Press pepper mixture with headspace measuring tool to remove any trapped air pockets. Add additional brine if necessary to maintain the ½-inch headspace.

5 Wipe the rim of each jar with a clean washcloth dipped in vinegar. Place a lid and ring on each jar and hand-tighten.

6 Place the jars in the water bather, ensuring each jar is covered by at least 1-inch of water. Bring the canner to a boil on high heat and process pints and half-pints for 15 minutes. Do not start your timer until the water is at a full rolling boil. After processing, wait 5 minutes before removing the jars from the canner.

Ingredient Tip

I like a lime slice to be seen on the side of the jar, so I will hold one slice against the interior of the jar when packing the jar with the pepper onion mixture, while the other lime rests on the bottom of the jar. Feel free to do so or place both lime slices on the bottom of each jar.

Pickled Seedless Grapes

MAKES APPROX. 4 QUARTS OR 8 PINTS

The warm tones of these pickled grapes give canners a variety of delicious uses. Use as a topping, fill fun desserts, garnish your favorite cocktail, or add life to a charcuterie board. Feel free to slice up a few to add to your fresh green salad or add several to spice up plain Greek yogurt.

5 cups apple cider vinegar

2 cup water

2 cups packed brown sugar

1 tablespoon pickling and canning salt

3 cinnamon sticks, halved

8 whole dried allspice berries

8 teaspoons mustard seed

8 teaspoons fresh gingerroot, peeled and finely chopped

9 cups seedless green or red grapes

1 In a large stainless steel stockpot, combine apple cider vinegar, water, brown sugar, salt, and cinnamon sticks. Bring to a boil over medium-high heat, stirring until sugar and salt have dissolved. Reduce heat and gently boil for 10 minutes to infuse the brine with the cinnamon. Remove from heat and discard cinnamon sticks.

2 In each quart jar, add 2 allspice berries, 2 teaspoons of mustard seeds, and 1 teaspoon gingerroot. If using pints, add one allspice berry, 1 teaspoon of mustard seeds, and a ½ teaspoon gingerroot. Remove the grapes from their stem and pack whole into jars leaving a generous 1-inch headspace.

3 Using a funnel, ladle hot pickling brine over grapes, filling to ½-inch headspace.

4 Gently tap each jar onto a cutting board to release trapped air pockets. Add additional brine if necessary to maintain the ½-inch headspace.

5 Wipe the rim of each jar with a clean washcloth dipped in vinegar. Place a lid and ring on each jar and hand-tighten.

6 Place the jars in the water bather, ensuring each jar is covered by at least 1-inch of water. Bring the canner to a boil on high heat and process pints and half-pints for 10 minutes. Do not start your timer until the water is at a full rolling boil. After processing, wait 5 minutes before removing the jars from the canner.

Pickled Serrano Peppers

MAKES APPROX. 6 PINTS

Excellent straight out of the jar or alongside a sandwich, you cannot go wrong with these spicy pickled peppers! This recipe is an excellent solution for home grown peppers whose yield was much higher than anticipated. Feel free to substitute serrano peppers with your favorite variety such as jalapeño, habanero, cayenne, or banana peppers.

6 cups white vinegar

2 cups water

½ cup pickling and canning salt

50-60 serrano peppers, whole

Seasonings per Jar

1 garlic clove

1 tablespoon black peppercorn

1 tablespoon coriander seeds

1 teaspoon cumin seeds

1 bay leaf

1 Brine: In a large stainless steel stockpot, combine vinegar, water and salt and bring to a boil over medium-high heat, stirring until salt is dissolved. Boil for 5 minutes then remove from heat.

2 In each pint jar add the garlic clove and dried seasoning, then tightly pack the serrano peppers, vine side up leaving a ½-inch headspace.

3 Using a funnel, ladle hot brine into jars leaving a ½-inch headspace. Gently tap each jar onto a cutting board to release trapped air pockets. Add additional brine if necessary to maintain the ½-inch headspace.

4 Wipe the rim of each jar with a clean wash cloth dipped in vinegar. Place a lid and ring on each jar and hand-tighten.

5 Place the jars in a water bather, ensuring each jar is covered by at least 1-inch of water. Bring the canner to a boil on high heat and process pint jars for 10 minutes. Do not start your timer until the water is at a full rolling boil. After processing, wait 5 minutes before removing the jars from the canner.

Pickled Beets and Onions

MAKES APPROX. 3 QUARTS OR 6 PINTS

One of my favorite snacks growing up as a child! I will always remember my mom using her favorite 1-gallon canning jar in her bright yellow kitchen to make this. She would make a large batch of pickled beets and onions, and later would add hard-boiled eggs after popping the top. By adding eggs, she would keep this jar of goodness in the fridge so we could enjoy this yummy snack any time!

3 tablespoons pickling spice

10 cups of prepared beets (10 to 12 medium)

2 ½ cups white vinegar

1 ½ cup water

1 cup sugar

2 large sweet onions, sliced or cut into rings

Cheesecloth and string

1 Using a 5-inch square piece of cheesecloth, place the pickling spice in the center. Tie together using string to create a spice bag. Set aside.

2 Leave 2-inches of green stem when cutting the fresh beet and keep the root intact. Blanch beets for 30 minutes in boiling water, then place immediately in a bowl of cold water in the sink. Under a cold stream of water from the faucet, use your thumbs and slide the skins off each beet.

3 On cutting board, remove beet stem and root and discard. Slice beets into ¼-inch rounds.

4 In a large, stainless steel stockpot, combine vinegar, water, sugar, onions, and spice bag. Bring to a boil over medium heat. Stir until sugar has dissolved and boil gently for 15 minutes. After 15 minutes, remove the spice bag and discard. Add prepared beets and onions, mix well, and return to a boil for 5 minutes.

5 Using a slotted spoon and funnel, ladle beets and onions into hot jars leaving a ¾-inch of headspace. Ladle hot pickling liquid over beets, filling to a ½-inch of headspace. Gently tap each jar onto a cutting board to release trapped air pockets. Add additional brine if necessary to maintain the ½-inch headspace.

6 Wipe the rim of each jar with a clean washcloth dipped in vinegar. Place a lid and ring on each jar and hand-tighten.

7 Place the jars in the water bather, ensuring each jar is covered by at least 2-inches of water. Bring the canner to a boil on high heat and process quarts and pints for 30 minutes. Do not start your timer until the water is at a full rolling boil. After processing, wait 5 minutes before removing the jars from the canner.

Dilly Beans

MAKES APPROX. 7 PINTS

Excellent in a salad, as an addition to any relish tray, or straight out of the jar! Pickled beans are all the rave. Have fun mixing the variety of beans to provide a variety of colors in each jar such as Kentucky Pole beans, yellow wax, royal burgundy, or purple string beans. Feel free to keep them dill flavored or add red pepper flakes to add some spice.

5 cups white vinegar

5 cups water

½ cup pickling or canning salt

14 pounds green beans

7 cloves of garlic, peeled and whole

3 ½ teaspoons dill seed or
14 fresh dill flower heads

3 ½ teaspoons mustard seed

3 ½ teaspoons red pepper flakes
(optional)

1 Brine: In a large, stainless steel stockpot, combine vinegar, water, and salt. Bring to a boil over medium-high heat and stir to dissolve the salt. Boil for 5 minutes then remove from heat and set aside.

2 Rinse beans in a colander and remove any discolored and disfigured beans from the lot. Using a cutting board and paring knife, remove the stem end of each bean. Cut the beans to the height of a pint jar, leaving room for 1-inch headspace.

3 In each pint jar place one garlic clove, ½ teaspoon dill seeds (or 2 fresh dill flower heads), ½ teaspoon mustard seeds, and a ½ teaspoon of hot pepper flakes. Tightly raw pack cut beans into each jar leaving a ¾-inch of headspace.

4 Using a funnel, ladle hot pickling liquid over beans, filling to a ½-inch of headspace. Gently tap each jar onto a cutting board to release trapped air pockets. Add additional brine if necessary to maintain the ½-inch headspace.

5 Wipe the rim of each jar with a clean washcloth dipped in vinegar. Place a lid and ring on each jar and hand-tighten.

6 Place the jars in the water bather, ensuring each jar is covered by at least 1-inch of water. Bring the canner to a boil on high heat and process pints for 10 minutes. Do not start your timer until the water is at a full rolling boil. After processing, wait 5 minutes before removing the jars from the canner.

Traditional Dill Pickles

To the Jar

MAKES APPROX. 7 PINTS

This is my family's favorite traditional dill pickle canning recipe on my pantry shelf. My daughter could eat a whole jar to herself. Be sure check out the Recipe Tip below if you are interested in turning this recipe into Easy Bread & Butter Pickles.

9 pounds pickling cucumber, whole or sliced (13 cups sliced)

3 tablespoons pickling spice

4 cups white vinegar

4 cups water

½ cup sugar

½ cup canning and pickling salt

7 fresh grape leaves

7 bay leaves

7 garlic cloves

2 tablespoons mustard seeds

14 heads of fresh dill flowers or 7 teaspoons dill seeds

1 Wash cucumbers to remove dirt and debris. If keeping whole, simply cut off the vine end of each cucumber. If slicing, cut into ¼-inch round pieces. Set aside.

2 Using a 5-inch square piece of cheesecloth, create a spice bag by placing the pickling spice in its center and tying the edges together.

3 In a large stainless steel stockpot, combine vinegar, water, sugar, salt, and the spice bag. Bring contents to a boil over medium-high heat, stirring often to dissolve the sugar and salt. Reduce heat and simmer on low for 15 minutes to infuse the spices into the brine.

4 Place 1 grape leaf, 1 bay leaf, 1 garlic clove, ½ teaspoon mustard seeds, and 2 dill flower heads (or 1 teaspoon of dill seeds) into each clean hot jar. Pack cucumbers into hot jars keeping a ½-inch of headspace.

5 Using a funnel, ladle hot brine over cucumbers, keeping the ½-inch headspace. Remove any air bubbles and add additional brine if necessary to maintain the ½-inch headspace.

6 Wipe each jar rim with a clean washcloth dipped in vinegar. Place a lid and ring on each jar and hand tighten.

7 Place jars in water bath, being sure each jar is covered with 1-inch of water. Bring to a boil and process pints for 10 minutes. Be sure not to start your timer until the water is at a full rolling boil. After processing, wait 5 minutes before removing the jars from the canner.

Ingredient Tip

Bread & Butter Pickles: Slice sweet onions to yield 6 cups and toss in with the sliced cucumbers. Switch white vinegar with apple cider vinegar and granulated sugar with 3 cups packed brown sugar. Remove the dill and replace with 2 tablespoons ground ginger and 1 tablespoon ground turmeric in the brine.

The Best Bloody Mary Mix

MAKES APPROX. 5 QUARTS OR 10 PINTS

The BEST Bloody Mary Mix in your pantry to accompany your pickled treats. When creating the mix, add a half-cup of pickling brine from an opened jar of one of your favorites to give this recipe a little something extra. If drinking alcohol is not your style, not to worry. This amazing mix replaces traditional tomato juice and is also an excellent starter when making stew.

45 medium tomatoes, any variety, cored and quartered

2 bell peppers, chopped (2 cups)

3 large carrots, peeled and diced (1 ½ cups)

1 large onion, diced (1 ½ cups)

2 celery stalks, diced (1 cup)

1 jalapeño, diced (½ cup)

8 garlic cloves, minced

½ cup fresh parsley leaves, coarsely chopped

½ cup bottled lemon juice

1½ tablespoons pickling and canning salt

1½ tablespoons Worcestershire sauce

2 teaspoons ground black pepper

2 teaspoons Tabasco® sauce

1 In a large stainless steel stockpot, add the quartered tomatoes, bell peppers, carrots, onion, celery, jalapeño, garlic, and parsley. Bring to a boil over medium-high heat, stirring often to avoid scorching. Reduce heat and simmer for 45 minutes until everything has softened.

2 Using a food processor and working in batches, purée the vegetables and set aside.

3 Press the mixture through a straining sieve, chinois, or food mill to remove seeds, skin, and pulp. Capture all the Bloody Mary mixture in a clean stockpot.

4 Add the lemon juice, salt, Worcestershire sauce, pepper, and Tabasco® sauce to the Bloody Mary Mix and mix well. Bring to a boil over medium-high heat for 5 minutes, stirring often.

5 Using a funnel, ladle hot mix into hot jars, leaving a 1-inch headspace.

6 Wipe the rim of each jar with a clean washcloth dipped in vinegar. Place a lid and ring on each jar and hand-tighten.

7 Place the jars in the pressure canner, lock the pressure canner lid, and bring the canner to a boil on high heat. Let the canner vent for 10 minutes. Process at 10 psi or according to your canner type and elevation. Process quarts and pints for 25 minutes.

8 Allow canner to return to zero psi before removing the canner lid. Wait 5 minutes before removing the jars from the canner.

CHAPTER 6

Meals in a Jar

With today's busy lifestyle, having a ready-made meal is essential to eating healthy while on the go. This chapter will give you a variety of recipes to help get a meal on the table in minutes. Enjoy preserving fun recipes such as White Chicken Chili, Chicken or Beef Fajitas, and Corned Beef Hash.

Chicken Pot Pie Filling

MAKES APPROX. 7 QUARTS OR 14 PINTS

Having my mom's delicious Chicken Pot Pie Filling on your pantry shelf aides in speedy, healthy meal creation. My kids love having it for dinner or as a quick weekend lunch. Feel free to open a quart to bake a traditional pot pie or simply serve the filling over freshly baked biscuits.

10 chicken breasts, boneless skinless (10 cups)

9 chicken thighs, boneless skinless (3 cups)

3 large bay leaves

4 stalks celery, chopped (2 cups)

3 medium onions, chopped (2 cups)

¼ cup butter

5 cups fresh or frozen chopped carrots

4 cups fresh or frozen peas

2 cups fresh or frozen corn kernels

1 tablespoon salt

2 teaspoons black pepper

2 teaspoons celery seeds

2 teaspoons garlic powder

8 cups chicken broth (store-bought or reserved)

1 ⅓ cups Canning Gel

1 Add chicken breasts, thighs and bay leaves to a large stockpot. Cover with three inches of water. Bring to a boil over medium high heat and cook for 15 minutes.

2 Reserve 8 cups of liquid if not using store-bought broth and reserve a separate 2 cups of liquid. Set aside.

3 Remove cooked chicken from boiled stockpot and set on a cutting board to cool. Remove bay leaves and discard. Chop or tear chicken into bite-sized pieces. Set aside or tear into bite-sized pieces and set aside.

4 In a large stainless steel stockpot, combine celery, onions, and butter. Sauté on medium heat until onions are translucent, about 8 minutes. Add carrots, peas, corn, chicken, salt, pepper, and 8 cups of broth to the onion mixture. Bring to a boil over medium-high heat, stirring well.

5 Whisk Canning Gel into ½ cup reserved broth and add to stockpot. Mix well. Boil pot pie filling for 5 additional minutes then remove from heat. If the pie filling becomes too thick during boiling, add an additional 1 to 2 cups of broth to thin out.

6 Using a funnel, ladle the filling into jars leaving a generous inch of headspace. Remove any air bubbles and add additional filling if necessary to maintain the generous inch of headspace.

7 Wipe the rim of each jar with a clean washcloth dipped in vinegar. Place a lid and ring on each jar and hand-tighten.

8 Place the jars in the pressure canner filled with 3 quarts of water, lock the pressure canner lid, and bring the canner to a boil on high heat. Let the canner vent for 10 minutes. Process at 10 psi or according to your canner type and elevation. Process quarts for 90 minutes and pints for 75 minutes. Allow canner to return to zero psi before removing the canner lid. Wait 5 minutes before removing the jars from the canner.

Corned Beef Hash

MAKES APPROX. 7 QUARTS OR 14 PINTS

Often called a "Depression era food," corned beef hash is a hearty mix of protein, carbs and fat for a filling stick-to-the-ribs meal. After canning your own from scratch, you'll likely never eat store-bought again!

7-8 pounds Corned beef (15-17 cups)

2 tablespoons pickling spice in a spice bag

¼ cup butter

2 large onions, chopped (3 cups)

5 pounds potatoes, cut into ½-inch cubes (10 cups)

2 tablespoons minced garlic

1 teaspoon black pepper

1 Rinse corned beef and place in a deep saucepan or stainless steel stockpot. Cover with water, add spice bag, and bring to a boil over medium-high heat. Reduce heat and cover, simmering for 40 minutes undisturbed. When done, remove corned beef and set on cutting board to cool. Discard water and spice bag.

2 Once cooled, cube the corned beef into ½-inch pieces. Set aside.

3 In a large stainless steel stockpot, add butter and onions, and cook over medium-high heat until onions are translucent, about 10 minutes. Add potatoes, corned beef, garlic, and black pepper, and mix well. Cook for an additional 5 minutes, stirring often to blend flavors and evenly disperse ingredients.

4 Using a funnel, ladle the hash into jars leaving a ½-inch of headspace. Remove air bubbles and add additional hash if necessary to maintain a ½-inch headspace.

5 Wipe the rim of each jar with a clean washcloth dipped in vinegar. Place a lid and ring on each jar and hand-tighten.

6 Place the jars in the pressure canner, lock the pressure canner lid, and bring the canner to a boil on high heat. Let the canner vent for 10 minutes. Process at 10 psi or according to your canner type and elevation. Process quarts for 90 minutes and pints for 75 minutes.

7 Allow canner to return to zero psi before removing the canner lid. Wait 5 minutes before removing the jars from the canner.

Ingredient Tip

You may also cook your corned beef in the crockpot overnight on low and shred your corned beef the next day before canning. The cubed versus shredded texture is a personal preference. Just know you may preserve it either way to suite your liking.

Beef Bourguignon

MAKES APPROX. 8 QUARTS

Delicacy in a jar! Once considered a peasant dish, over time it has become a standard in French cuisine. Oh, and did I mention it tastes absolutely delicious? Julia Child described this dish as "certainly one of the most delicious beef dishes concocted by man." Serve it over roasted garlic mashed potatoes.

6 pounds chuck roast, cut into 2-inch chunks (12 cups)

½ cup extra-virgin olive oil, divided

12 ounces thick-cut bacon, cut into ½-inch pieces

½ cup garlic cloves, smashed with knife blade

6 medium onions, coarsely chopped (3 cups)

18 shallots, peeled and sliced longways (3 cups)

3 pounds quartered white mushrooms (15 cups)

1 tablespoon salt

1 ½ teaspoons black pepper

2 bottles of burgundy wine (Merlot, Malbec, Pinot Noir, or Chianti)

2 cups beef stock

1 cup cognac

10 carrots, peeled and cut into 2-inch chunks (5 cups)

1 Pat beef dry with a paper towel so beef will brown properly. In a large skillet, quickly brown the cubed beef in batches using a tablespoon of olive oil at a time. Brown all sides, but move quickly. You do not want to fully cook the beef. After all the beef chunks are browned, set inside in a large stockpot.

2 In the skillet with all the beef renderings, add the bacon, garlic, and remaining olive oil. Cook over medium heat until bacon is done but not crisp.

3 Using the same skillet, add onions, shallots, mushrooms, salt, and pepper and sauté until onions are translucent, about 8 minutes. Place into the large stockpot with the browned beef and bacon. Be sure to scrape every dripping from the skillet into the stockpot. Mix well.

4 Add both bottles of wine and the cognac. Bring mixture to a boil on medium-high heat, stirring often. Once at a boil, reduce heat and simmer on low for one hour. Stir often to avoid scorching. After one hour, add carrots and simmer for another hour. Be sure to taste test and add additional salt and pepper, as needed.

5 Using a funnel, ladle the bourguignon into jars leaving a generous inch of headspace. Remove air bubbles and add additional bourguignon if necessary to maintain a generous inch of headspace.

6 Wipe the rim of each jar with a clean washcloth dipped in vinegar. Place a lid and ring on each jar and hand-tighten.

7 Place the jars in the pressure canner filled with 3 quarts of water, lock the pressure canner lid, and bring the canner to a boil on high heat. Let the canner vent for 10 minutes. Process at 10 psi or according to your canner type and elevation. Process quarts for 90 minutes and pints for 75 minutes.

8 Allow canner to return to zero psi before removing the canner lid. Wait 5 minutes before removing the jars from the canner.

Chili con Carne

MAKES APPROX. 10 QUARTS OR 20 PINTS

To the Jar

No matter the season, it is sheer delight having this hearty meal sitting on your pantry shelf. Entertaining guests? Cut out the interior of a round loaf of bread making an edible bread bowl, heat up a quart or two, pour it in your bread bowl, and serve hot.

½ pound dried black beans (1 cup)
½ pound dried kidney beans (1 cup)
¼ pound dried pinto beans (1/2 cup)
5 pounds of ground beef
2 pounds ground Italian sausage
2 large onions, chopped (2 cups)
2 bell peppers, chopped (2 cups)
1 jalapeño, deseeded and finely chopped (½ cup)
4 large stalks parsley, finely chopped (½ cup loosely packed)
36 medium Roma tomatoes, chopped (12 cups)
1 cup chili powder
¼ cup cumin powder
5-8 garlic cloves, minced
1 teaspoon cumin seeds
1-2 teaspoons red pepper flakes
6-8 drops Tabasco® sauce (optional)
1 tablespoon salt
¼ teaspoon black pepper

1 Rinse and sort the dried beans in a large colander being sure to remove any debris, rocks, and disfigured beans. Next, place cleaned dried beans in a large stockpot and cover with water. Bring to a boil over medium-high heat and boil hard for 2 minutes, stirring often. Remove from heat, cover, and let soak for 1 hour.

2 Brown ground beef and sausage in a large, thick-bottomed stockpot. Remove excess grease. Add onions, bell peppers, jalapeño, and parsley to the meat mixture and mix well. Cook on medium-high heat until onions are translucent, about 8 minutes.

3 Drain beans in colander, give them a quick rinse and shake off excess water. Add the beans and tomatoes to the stockpot and mix well. Bring contents to a boil on medium-high heat, stirring often to avoid scorching. Add chili powder, ground cumin, cumin seeds, red pepper flakes, Tabasco® sauce, salt, and pepper. Reduce heat and boil gently for 15 minutes, stirring often.

4 Using a funnel, ladle the chili into jars leaving a 1-inch of headspace. Remove air bubbles and add additional chili if necessary to maintain a 1-inch headspace.

5 Wipe the rim of each jar with a clean washcloth dipped in vinegar. Place a lid and ring on each jar and hand-tighten.

6 Place the jars in the pressure canner, lock the pressure canner lid, and bring the canner to a boil on high heat. Let the canner vent for 10 minutes. Process at 10 psi or according to your canner type and elevation. Process quarts for 90 minutes and pints for 75 minutes.

7 Allow canner to return to zero psi before removing the canner lid. Wait 5 minutes before removing the jars from the canner.

Mumma Newton's Homemade Chicken Soup

MAKES APPROX. 8 QUARTS OR 16 PINTS

This is a staple in my pantry, especially during cold and flu season. I consider this family recipe Nature's Penicillin! If you have soup liquid remaining, do not toss it. Fill your jars with soup liquid and process them right alongside the soup in your pressure canner. Doing so will give you jars of chicken stock to use in future meal creations.

8 quarts of water (32 cups)

1 whole chicken, including carcass and skin (remove innards and neck bone)

3 bay leaves

12 carrots, chopped (6 cups)

4 medium onions, diced (2 cups)

4 celery stalks, chopped (2 cups)

3 large Idaho or Russet potatoes, cut into 1-inch cubes (2 cups)

1 pint Basil Diced Tomatoes (page 75) or 4 large tomatoes and 1 bell pepper, diced

5 garlic cloves, chopped fine

1 tablespoon crushed basil leaves

1 tablespoon salt

2 teaspoons black pepper

1 Place water, chicken, and bay leaves in a large stockpot and bring to boil over medium-high heat. Reduce heat to medium and boil chicken until cooked through, approximately 30 minutes. Be sure to stir chicken often to avoid scorching. Skim off any foam and discard. Once cooked through, remove chicken and set aside on cutting board to cool. Keep the water in the stockpot because it is the soup base.

2 Remove all skin and bones from chicken. Using either a knife or your fingers, cut or tear all the chicken into bite-size pieces. Add cut chicken back to stockpot.

3 Add carrots, celery, onions, potatoes, and one pint Basil Diced Tomatoes (or 4 diced tomatoes and 1 diced bell pepper) to the stockpot. Bring to a boil over medium-high heat, stirring often, and cook for 5 minutes. Remove from heat.

4 Using a funnel and slotted spoon, fill each jar ¾ full with chicken and vegetables. Next, ladle soup broth into jars leaving a 1-inch of headspace.

5 Wipe the rim of each jar with a clean washcloth dipped in vinegar. Place a lid and ring on each jar and hand-tighten.

6 Place the jars in the pressure canner filled with 3 quarts of water, lock the pressure canner lid, and bring the canner to a boil on high heat. Let the canner vent for 10 minutes. Process at 10 psi or according to your canner type and elevation. Process quarts for 90 minutes and pints for 75 minutes.

7 Allow canner to return to zero psi before removing the canner lid. Wait 5 minutes before removing the jars from the canner.

Ingredient Tip

Feel free to use a pint jar of your favorite home canned salsa in place of Basil Diced Tomatoes. It will give your soup the zip it needs and the jalapeños will help you sweat out the crud. Also, if you do not have access to a whole chicken, use 2 large bone-in breasts with rib meat and 2 chicken thighs to make the soup.

White Chicken Chili

MAKES APPROX. 7 QUARTS OR 14 PINTS

This hearty chili uses broth, white beans, and chicken living up to its name. Flavored with green chilis and cumin, you will have a new fall favorite stored in your pantry.

2 tablespoons extra-virgin olive oil

6 large chicken breasts, boneless skinless, chopped (6 cups)

9 chicken thighs, boneless skinless, chopped (3 cups)

1 large red onion, chopped (1 ½ cups)

2 jalapeños, finely chopped (1 cup)

6 garlic cloves, minced (2 tablespoons)

1 cup green chiles, finely chopped or one 7-ounce store-bought can

12 cups chicken broth

4 cups water

1 cup bottled lime juice

¼ cup ground cumin

1 tablespoon dried oregano

2 teaspoons paprika

2 teaspoons ground coriander

2 pint jars of cannellini, navy, or northern beans (page 79) or 2 store-bought cans, drained and rinsed

2 cups corn kernels, frozen or fresh

½ cup fresh cilantro, coarsely chopped (optional)

1 In a large stainless steel stockpot, heat oil on medium-high. Then, add chopped chicken and toss to coat. Cook for 10 minutes. Add red onion, jalapeño, garlic, and green chiles and continue to cook for 5 minutes.

2 Add chicken broth, water, lime juice, oregano, paprika, coriander, and beans. Reduce heat and gently boil for 20 minutes, stirring often. Add corn and cilantro and cook for an additional 5 minutes, then remove from heat.

3 Using a funnel, ladle the chili into jars leaving a 1-inch of headspace.

4 Wipe the rim of each jar with a clean washcloth dipped in vinegar. Place a lid and ring on each jar and hand-tighten.

5 Place the jars in the pressure canner filled with 3 quarts of water, lock the pressure canner lid, and bring the canner to a boil on high heat. Let the canner vent for 10 minutes. Process at 10 psi or according to your canner type and elevation. Process quarts for 90 minutes and pints for 75 minutes.

6 Allow canner to return to zero psi before removing the canner lid. Wait 5 minutes before removing the jars from the canner.

To the Jar

Jambalaya

MAKES APPROX. 9 QUARTS OR 18 PINTS

This recipe is a classic creole southern dish with shrimp, chicken, and andouille sausage. Its hearty helping of vegetables and authentic Cajun spices make this meal in a jar a special treat to serve any time of the year. Add a pint of home canned Cajun Holy Trinity (page 68) when making this recipe. When ready to eat, simply empty a quart jar into a saucepan, add ½ cup white rice, and cook on medium heat until rice is done.

8 chicken breasts, bone in and skin on (8 cups)

8 cups water

3 bay leaves

2 tablespoons extra-virgin olive oil

32-ounces Andouille sausage, sliced into ¼-inch thick rounds (4 cups)

1 ½ pounds raw shrimp, peeled and deveined (3 cups)

16 Roma tomatoes, diced (4 cups)

2 cups sliced okra, fresh or frozen

1 large onion, chopped (1 ½ cups)

1 red bell pepper, chopped (1 cup)

1 green bell pepper, chopped (1 cup)

2 jalapeños, finely chopped (1 cup)

2 celery stalks, finely chopped (1 cup)

½ cup fresh parsley, coarsely chopped and loosely packed

16 garlic cloves, minced (4 tablespoons)

8 cups chicken stock

4 tablespoons Tony Chachere's creole mix

1 tablespoon dried oregano

2 teaspoons dried thyme

2 teaspoons paprika

1 Combine chicken, water and bay leaves in a large stockpot. Bring to a boil over medium-high heat and cook for 30 minutes, mixing often. Remove chicken from stockpot to cool, discard bay leaves, and keep liquid simmering. Cut or tear chicken into 2-inch pieces and add to stockpot.

2 In a skillet, add olive oil and andouille sausage and toss to coat. Over medium-high heat, lightly brown both sides, about 8 minutes. Remove cooked sausage from skillet and place into stockpot. Add shrimp to cooking liquid. Over medium-high heat, bring stockpot to boil.

3 Add tomatoes, okra, onions, bell peppers, jalapeños, celery, parsley, and garlic to the stockpot, mix well and cook for 8 minutes or until onions are soft. Add chicken stock, Tony's creole seasoning mix, oregano, thyme and paprika, and mix well. Cook for an additional 5 minutes.

4 Using a funnel and slotted spoon, fill each jar ¾ full of meat and vegetable mixture. Next, ladle jambalaya liquid into jars leaving a generous inch of headspace. Remove air bubbles and add additional liquid if necessary to maintain a generous inch of headspace.

5 Wipe the rim of each jar with a clean washcloth dipped in vinegar. Place a lid and ring on each jar and hand-tighten.

6 Place the jars in the pressure canner, lock the pressure canner lid, and bring the canner to a boil on high heat. Let the canner vent for 10 minutes. Process at 10 psi or according to your canner type and elevation. Process quarts for 90 minutes and pints for 75 minutes.

7 Allow canner to return to zero psi before removing the canner lid. Wait 5 minutes before removing the jars from the canner.

Recipe Tip

If you have left over Jambalaya cooking liquid, be sure to fill a few pint jars and pressure can it right alongside jars filled with Jambalaya. You can use this flavorful liquid instead of broth or water to make rice or couscous in the future.

Mediterranean Chicken

To the Jar

MAKES APPROX. 5 QUARTS OR 10 PINTS

Mediterranean cuisine may not be a product of a specific culture but is a label referred to the culinary trends shared by a diverse array of people who live in the region around the Mediterranean Sea. A common element are recipes dominated by vegetables and incorporating olives. Have fun creating this deliciously flavored meal in a jar to enjoy any time of the year.

2 tablespoons extra-virgin olive oil

20 chicken thighs, boneless skinless

8 shallots, peeled and sliced thin (2 ½ cups)

12 garlic cloves, minced (3 tablespoons)

9 medium artichoke hearts

6 carrots, rough chopped (3 cups)

½ pound white button mushrooms, chopped (2 ¾ cups)

2 cups Kalamata olives

3 lemons, cut into 1-inch thick slices then cut in half

4 cups chicken stock

2 cups white wine (Chardonnay or Pino Grigio)

2 cups cherry tomatoes

4 sprigs fresh thyme

4 sprigs fresh oregano

2 teaspoons salt

1 teaspoon black pepper

1 teaspoon smoked paprika

1 Working in batches in a stainless steel stockpot on medium-high heat, add 1 tablespoon of oil and chicken thighs. Cook until browned, about 5 minutes, then flip and brown the other side. Repeat until all chicken thighs are browned. Set aside.

2 Add shallots and garlic to stockpot and cook until shallots are soft, about 5 minutes. Add artichoke hearts, carrots, mushrooms, olives, and lemons. Mix well and cook for 5 minutes to blend flavors.

Next, add chicken stock, white wine, cherry tomatoes, thyme, oregano, salt pepper, and paprika. Stir to blend flavors. Bring to a boil, then add the chicken thighs atop the mixture. Reduce heat to low, cover with lid and braise for 10 minutes.

3 Remove thyme and oregano sprigs from stockpot and discard. Then, using tongs and warm jars, add 4 chicken thighs to each quart jar. If using pints, add 2 chicken thighs to each jar.

4 Using a funnel and slotted spoon, equally disperse the vegetables, olives, and artichoke hearts into each jar. Next, ladle the sauce into jars leaving a 1-inch of headspace. Remove air bubbles and add additional sauce if necessary to maintain a 1-inch headspace.

5 Wipe the rim of each jar with a clean washcloth dipped in vinegar. Place a lid and ring on each jar and hand-tighten.

6 Place the jars in the pressure canner, lock the pressure canner lid, and bring the canner to a boil on high heat. Let the canner vent for 10 minutes. Process at 10 psi or according to your canner type and elevation. Process quarts for 90 minutes and pints for 75 minutes.

7 Allow canner to return to zero psi before removing the canner lid. Wait 5 minutes before removing the jars from the canner.

If you wish to substitute pork over chicken

Ingredient Tip

like they do in Southern European cuisine, feel free to use a 2 ½-pound pork tenderloin sliced into ½-inch thick slices, then braise just as the chicken thighs.

Chicken Tortilla Soup

MAKES APPROX. 7 QUARTS OR 14 PINTS

This authentic flavored soup has amazing body and boasts delicious flavor. Top each bowl with thin tortilla strips, shredded cheese, a dollop of sour cream, and dash of hot sauce.

8 chicken breasts (8 cups)

12 chicken thighs (4 cups)

16 Roma tomatoes, diced (5 ½ cups)

4 cups fresh or frozen corn kernels

3 pints home canned black beans (page 79) or 3 15-ounce store-bought cans

3 large carrots, sliced ½-inch
(1 ½ cups)

1 large Vidalia onion, diced

1 cup mild green chilies, chopped fine or 7 ounces store bought

4 cups water

10 cups chicken stock

10 garlic cloves, minced

2 tablespoon ground cumin

2 tablespoon ground chili powder

1 tablespoon salt

1 tablespoon dried oregano

2 teaspoons paprika

2-4 dried cayenne peppers

2 tablespoons Canning Gel

1 In a small stockpot, cover chicken breasts and thighs with 2-inches of water and bring to a boil over medium-high heat. Cook for 15 minutes. Remove chicken and set aside to cool. Shred or cut into bite size pieces. Discard water or season and can in jars alongside soup as a simple broth to use later in meal creations.

2 In a large stockpot, combine chopped chicken, tomatoes, corn, black beans, carrots, onions, chilies, water, chicken stock, garlic, cumin, chili powder, salt, oregano, paprika, and dried cayenne peppers. Bring to a boil over medium-high heat, stirring often. Reduce heat and simmer for 10 minutes. Remove dried cayenne peppers from soup and discard. Whisk in the Canning Gel then remove from heat.

3 Using a slotted spoon and funnel, fill hot jars to a generous inch of headspace with soup contents. Next, ladle soup broth filling to 1-inch of headspace.

4 Wipe the rim of each jar with a clean washcloth dipped in vinegar. Place a lid and ring on each jar and hand-tighten.

5 Place the jars in the pressure canner filled with 3 quarts of water, lock the pressure canner lid, and bring the canner to a boil on high heat. Let the canner vent for 10 minutes. Process at 10 psi or according to your canner type and elevation. Process quarts for 90 minutes and pints for 75 minutes.

6 Allow canner to return to zero psi before removing the canner lid. Wait 5 minutes before removing the jars from the canner.

Spaghetti Sauces

Makes approx. 14 pints or 7 quarts

Zesty Spaghetti Sauce

30 pounds Roma tomatoes approx. a half-bushel

14 dried California chili peppers

1 ½ pounds ground beef

1 ½ pounds Italian sausage

1 ½ cups onions, chopped

1 cup green pepper, seeded and chopped

5 tablespoons garlic, minced

6 tablespoons fresh parsley, coarsely chopped

4 tablespoons fresh basil

½ cup packed brown sugar

2 tablespoons dried oregano

4 teaspoons sea salt

3 teaspoons black pepper

Garden Spaghetti Sauce

30 pounds Roma tomatoes, approx. a half-bushel

3 cups carrots, finely chopped

3 cups zucchini, shredded

1 cup summer squash, shredded

1 celery stalk, finely chopped

1 ½ cups onions, chopped

1 cup green pepper, seeded and chopped

½ pound mushrooms, sliced (optional)

5 tablespoons garlic, minced

6 tablespoons fresh parsley, coarsely chopped

4 tablespoons fresh basil

½ cup packed brown sugar

2 tablespoons dried oregano

4 teaspoons sea salt

Traditional Spaghetti Sauce

30 pounds Roma tomatoes, approx. a half-bushel

1 ½ pounds ground beef

1 ½ pounds Italian sausage

1 ½ cups onions, chopped

1 cup green pepper, seeded and chopped

½ pound mushrooms, sliced (optional)

5 tablespoons garlic, minced

6 tablespoons fresh parsley, coarsely chopped

4 tablespoons fresh basil

½ cup packed brown sugar

2 tablespoons dried oregano

4 teaspoons sea salt

3 teaspoons black pepper

199

These are my go-to jars when making a variety of meals that require a red sauce base. There are three different varieties – traditional, zesty, and a meatless garden blend. Each variety exemplifies three different flavors. The benefit of having three different sauces is you never tire of using red sauce, because you now have options to choose from based on your mood, your taste buds, and the meal being created.

1 **Tomato Prep:** Core and cut tomatoes into quarters and purée in a food processor. Place purée in a large, thick-bottomed stainless steel stockpot. Bring to a boil over medium-high heat, stirring frequently to avoid scorching. Once to a boil, reduce heat and boil gently for 10 minutes. Remove from heat and set aside.

2 Follow the information below according to the spaghetti sauce you will be preparing.

Chili Purée (for Zesty Spaghetti Sauce): Remove stems and place in a stainless steel bowl. Cover dried peppers with boiling water and submerge for 20 minutes. To fully submerge the peppers, place a salad plate atop the peppers, fill a soup bowl with hot water and place on top of the plate. Once rehydrated, place reconstituted chilies and a ½ cup of the liquid into your food processor and purée. Set aside.

Meat/Spices (for Traditional & Zesty Spaghetti Sauces): In a skillet, cook sausage and ground beef until done. Drain excess fat. Add onions, green peppers, garlic, mushrooms, parsley, basil, oregano, salt, and black pepper. Cook on medium heat until onions are clear and peppers are soft.

Vegetables/Spices (for Garden Spaghetti Sauce): In a skillet, add onions, green peppers, garlic, mushrooms, parsley, basil, oregano, salt, and black pepper. Cook on medium heat until onions are clear and peppers are soft. Add remaining vegetables, mix well, and cook for 5 minutes to blend flavors.

3 Add the meat, vegetable, or chili purée to the tomatoes. Stir in brown sugar, then bring to a boil over medium-high heat. Boil gently for 5 minutes, stirring often.

4 Using a funnel, ladle sauce into jars leaving a 1-inch of headspace.

5 Wipe the rim of each jar with a clean washcloth dipped in vinegar. Place a lid and ring on each jar and hand-tighten.

6 Place the jars in the pressure canner filled with 3 quarts of water, lock the pressure canner lid, and bring the canner to a boil on high heat. Let the canner vent for 10 minutes. Process at 10 psi or according to your canner type and elevation. Process quarts for 70 minutes and pints for 60 minutes.

7 Allow canner to return to zero psi before removing the canner lid. Wait 5 minutes before removing the jars from the canner.

Ingredient Tip

I have learned it takes approximately 18 average-sized Roma tomatoes to equal 8 cups of food-processed tomatoes. Also, the skin of a Roma tomato is very thin and can be used in canning recipes without blanching. Traditional canning tomatoes should be blanched with the skins removed when used to make sauce.

Hearty Meatball Recipe

MAKES APPROX. 5 SERVINGS

This recipe makes a juicy meatball packed with tons of flavor, suitable for any spaghetti sauce. Feel free to use this delicious meatball recipe in other fun ways such as a new addition to your french onion soup, atop your favorite homemade pizza, as a scrumptious addition to Hawaiian Sausage Appetizer (page 96), or cover the meatballs with your favorite sauce to enjoy during a football game. The possibilities are endless!

1 pound lean ground beef

½ pound Italian sausage

2 eggs, beaten

¼ cup milk

3 slices Italian bread, ripped into tiny pieces

1 small onion, finely chopped

3 garlic cloves, minced

2 tablespoons fresh parsley, finely chopped

1 tablespoon Worcestershire sauce

¼ teaspoon black pepper

½ cup grated Romano cheese

1 Preheat oven to 400°F. Line a baking sheet with foil and spray with non-stick cooking oil.

2 In a large bowl, crack eggs and beat well. Add milk and beat together with fork. Add bread pieces, onions, garlic, parsley, Worcestershire sauce, and black pepper, and mix well to evenly coat.

3 Using your hands, crumble the ground beef and sausage into the egg mixture. Add grated Romano cheese and blend well.

4 Shape meat mixture into 1 ½-inch to 2-inch round balls, rolling each in the palm of your hands. Or, use a cookie scoop to keep the meatball sizes uniform. Place on lined cookie sheet and bake uncovered for 10 minutes, then flip meatballs over and bake for an additional 10 minutes. Remove from oven and use in your recipe or cool before storing in the freezer. These will last 3 months frozen.

Recipe Tip

If you would like to create a spaghetti dinner using this meatball recipe, gather 1 quart of your favorite Spaghetti Sauce (page 197) and 1 half-pint jar tomato paste (8 ounces). Heat sauce in a saucepan over medium heat and stir in the tomato paste. Simmer to thicken. Add meatballs, cook for 5 additional minutes, and serve hot over spaghetti.

Stuffed Shells

MAKES APPROX. 8 TO 10 SERVINGS

To the Table

This is a very popular recipe in my home – and a perfect dinner for entertaining guests. Loaded with authentic Italian ingredients, these beautiful stuffed shells are the perfect way to highlight any of my three home canned spaghetti sauce recipes. This recipe may also be frozen up to 3 months. Simply thaw it in the refrigerator overnight and bake according to instructions.

25-30 jumbo pasta shells

1 pound Italian sausage

1 medium onion, finely chopped

4 garlic cloves, minced

6-8 white button mushrooms, finely chopped

2 cups fresh spinach leaves, finely chopped or 1 10-ounce frozen package

15 ounces Ricotta cheese

1 large egg, beaten

1 teaspoon sea salt

½ teaspoon black pepper

2 cups grated Romano cheese, divided

1 cup Mozzarella cheese, divided

1 quart jar Garden, Traditional or Zesty Spaghetti sauce (page 197)

1 Preheat oven to 375° F.

2 Bring a large stockpot of lightly salted water to boil. Add shells one at a time to avoid shells from nesting and sticking together. Return to a boil, then cover, and remove from heat. Let stand 10 minutes then drain and rinse with hot water. Set aside.

3 Cook sausage in a skillet for 5 minutes, breaking apart any clumps. Add onions, garlic, and mushrooms and cook until onions are translucent. Add spinach and cook until wilted. Remove from heat to cool.

4 In a large mixing bowl, combine Ricotta cheese, egg, salt, pepper, 1 cup Romano cheese, and ½ cup Mozzarella cheese. Mix well. Add the cooled sausage mixture and stir until evenly combined. Set aside.

5 In a medium-sized pot, warm spaghetti sauce through on medium-high heat. Using a 13x9 baking dish, spread 1 cup spaghetti sauce across the bottom of the dish.

6 Fill each shell with 3 to 4 tablespoons of the sausage mixture and set upright in the baking dish. After your dish is filled with stuffed shells, dabble a spoonful of spaghetti sauce atop each shell.

7 Cover with foil and bake for 25 minutes, or until sauce is bubbling. Remove foil and sprinkle the remaining cheeses overtop. Return to oven and bake uncovered for 8 to 10 minutes, or until cheese is melted. Serve with additional spaghetti sauce and a side salad.

205

Beef Stew with Vegetables

MAKES APPROX. 7 QUARTS

This hearty meal is sure to please. It is best enjoyed alongside freshly baked bread or over roasted garlic mashed potatoes after being thickened with 3 tablespoons of Canning Gel.

2 tablespoons extra virgin olive oil

5 pounds of stewing beef, cut in 1 ½-inch cubes

6 pounds potatoes, peeled and cubed (12 cups)

16 carrots, peeled and chopped (8 cups)

6 celery stalks, chopped (3 cups)

2 large onions, chopped (3 cups)

1 pint jar Basil Diced Tomatoes (page 75) or 6 Roma tomatoes, diced (2 cups)

1 tablespoon dried parsley flakes

1 tablespoon dried oregano

1 tablespoon salt

½ tablespoon celery seed

1 teaspoon ground coriander

1 teaspoon dried thyme

1 teaspoon dried basil

½ teaspoons ground black pepper

8 cups beef broth

5 cups boiling water

2 beef bouillon cubes (optional)

1 In a large skillet, brown beef in batches, using one tablespoon of oil olive at a time. Be sure not to cook the meat, just simply brown each side and remove from skillet. Transfer the browned beef and drippings from the skillet and into a large, thick-bottomed stainless steel stockpot.

2 Add potatoes, carrots, celery, onions, tomatoes, parsley, oregano, salt, celery seed, coriander, thyme, basil, and black pepper to the stockpot. Mix well. Add beef broth, water, and bouillon cubes, to the stockpot. Stir together and bring to a boil over medium-high heat. Once at a boil, reduce heat and gently boil for 5 minutes.

3 Using a funnel, ladle the stew into jars leaving a 1-inch of headspace. Remove any air bubbles and add additional stew if necessary to maintain the 1-inch headspace.

4 Wipe the rim of each jar with a clean washcloth dipped in vinegar. Place a lid and ring on each jar and hand-tighten.

5 Place the jars in the pressure canner filled with 3 quarts of water, lock the pressure canner lid, and bring the canner to a boil on high heat. Let the canner vent for 10 minutes. Process at 10 psi or according to your canner type and elevation. Process quarts for 90 minutes and pints for 75 minutes.

6 Allow canner to return to zero psi before removing the canner lid. Wait 5 minutes before removing the jars from the canner.

Roasted Poblano Corn Chowder

MAKES APPROX. 3 QUARTS OR 6 PINTS

This quickly became one of my family's favorites thanks to the amazing flavor profile from the roasted poblanos, coriander, spices, and hearty texture. When ready to heat a quart jar, simply add ½ cup of heavy cream, 1 cup of shredded cheddar cheese, and top with chopped cilantro. Perfection!

9 large poblano peppers

6 cups vegetable, or chicken, broth

3 large Yukon gold potatoes, cut into 1-inch cubes (4 cups)

4 cups corn kernels, fresh or frozen

3 medium yellow onions, chopped (1½ cups)

1 celery stalk, chopped (½ cup)

4 garlic cloves, minced (2 tablespoons)

3 bay leaves

2 teaspoons ground cumin

1 ½ teaspoons ground coriander

1 teaspoon oregano

1 teaspoon salt

¼ teaspoon black pepper

1 Roast poblano peppers on an aluminum foil lined baking sheet under the oven broiler for 8 minutes or until the skin starts to blister and blacken. Using tongs, carefully flip the peppers to blacken the other side, about 5 minutes. Remove poblanos from oven and let cool to the touch. Pull off as much skin as the pepper allows, being sure to leave some blistered skin for flavor. Cut the poblanos open on a cutting board and remove the stem and seeds. Dice the poblanos and place in large stainless steel stockpot.

2 Add the vegetable broth to the stockpot with the poblanos and bring to a boil over medium-high heat. Add the potatoes, corn, onions, celery, garlic, bay leaves, cumin, coriander, oregano, salt, and pepper. Mix well.

3 Using a funnel, ladle the chowder into jars leaving a 1-inch of headspace. Remove air bubbles and add additional chowder if necessary to maintain a 1-inch headspace.

4 Wipe the rim of each jar with a clean washcloth dipped in vinegar. Place a lid and ring on each jar and hand-tighten.

5 Place the jars in the pressure canner, lock the pressure canner lid, and bring the canner to a boil on high heat. Let the canner vent for 10 minutes. Process at 10 psi or according to your canner type and elevation. Process quarts for 85 minutes and pints for 55 minutes.

6 Allow canner to return to zero psi before removing the canner lid. Wait 5 minutes before removing the jars from the canner.

209

Beef Tips & Gravy with Whole Garlic Cloves

To the Jar

MAKES APPROX. 6 TO 8 PINTS

Having jars of this protein-packed meat on the ready will make excellent meal starters! Reheat this seasoned, cooked meat and serve alongside vegetables, atop mashed potatoes, or mix with cooked egg noodles for a quick meal. You may also use these scrumptious bits when making soups and stews.

10-12 pounds stew beef

8-16 garlic whole cloves

2-4 tablespoons of extra virgin olive oil

2 teaspoons sea salt

1 teaspoon black pepper

4 cups hot water

½ cup Canning Gel

1 Choose the highest cut of meat you prefer to eat. Trim away gristle, remove excess fat, and sliver skin and any bruising. Cut meat into 1- to 2-inch thick chunks, cubes, or strips, depending on your liking.

2 Pat your meat dry with paper towel so it will brown properly. In a deep skillet, sear the meat in batches using 1 tablespoon of olive oil per batch. Dash each batch with sea salt and black pepper. Work quickly, searing on all sides for only a few seconds. Do not to cook the meat. Set aside. Leave the drippings in the skillet.

3 Add 4 cups of hot water to skillet. Whisk in Canning Gel and bring liquid mixture to a quick boil, stirring frequently. Boil for 2 minutes then remove from heat. Set aside.

4 Add 1-2 whole garlic cloves to each warm jar. Pack meat chunks into each jar, leaving a generous inch headspace. Ladle hot gravy mixture over top of meat being sure to keep the generous inch headspace. Remove air bubbles using your bubble remover tool and add more gravy if necessary to maintain the headspace.

5 Wipe the rim of each jar with a clean washcloth dipped in vinegar. Place a lid and ring on each jar and hand-tighten.

6 Place the jars in the pressure canner filled with 3 quarts of water, lock the pressure canner lid, and bring the canner to a boil on high heat. Let the canner vent for 10 minutes. Process at 10 psi or according to your canner type and elevation. Process quarts for 90 minutes and pints for 75 minutes.

7 Allow canner to return to zero psi before removing the canner lid. Wait 5 minutes before removing the jars from the canner.

Pulled Mexican Chicken

To the Jar

MAKES APPROX. 6 QUARTS OR 12 PINTS

The authentic flavors of pulled Mexican chicken will put a smile on everyone's face and fill their bellies with a hearty helping of pulled chicken and peppers.

12 chicken breasts, boneless skinless (15 cups shredded)

12 Roma tomatoes, diced (4 cups)

3 red bell peppers, deseeded and chopped (3 cups)

1 large Vidalia onion, chopped (1 ½ cups)

6 garlic cloves, minced (3 tablespoons)

4 tablespoon apple cider vinegar

4 tablespoons Agave sweetener

¼ cup chili powder

2 tablespoons yellow mustard

2 tablespoons dried oregano

2 tablespoons ground coriander

2 tablespoons your favorite hot sauce (I like Valentinos)

2 teaspoons onion powder

2 tablespoons ground cumin

6 ounces tomato paste

1 In a large stockpot, add chicken breasts and cover with two inches of water. Bring to a boil over medium-high heat and cook for 25 minutes. Using tongs, place cooked chicken onto a cutting board to cool. Shred the chicken and set aside. Discard cooking liquid unless you would like to season it and can it in jars to process alongside the pulled chicken.

2 In a clean large stockpot, add the tomatoes, bell peppers, onion, garlic, apple cider vinegar, and agave and mix well. Cook for 10 minutes on medium heat, stirring often to avoid scorching. Add shredded chicken and proceed to cook on medium heat.

3 Add chili powder, mustard, oregano, coriander, hot sauce, onion powder, and cumin. Mix well to blend ingredients and bring to a boil over medium-high heat. Once at a boil, mix in the tomato paste and continue mixing until the paste has evenly dispersed, about 5 minutes.

4 Using a funnel, ladle the mixture into jars leaving a 1-inch of headspace. Remove any air bubbles and add additional mixture if necessary to maintain the 1-inch headspace.

5 Wipe the rim of each jar with a clean washcloth dipped in vinegar. Place a lid and ring on each jar and hand-tighten.

6 Place the jars in the pressure canner filled with 3 quarts of water, lock the pressure canner lid, and bring the canner to a boil on high heat. Let the canner vent for 10 minutes. Process at 10 psi or according to your canner type and elevation. Process quarts for 90 minutes and pints for 75 minutes.

7 Allow canner to return to zero psi before removing the canner lid. Wait 5 minutes before removing the jars from the canner.

Borscht aka Beet Soup

MAKES APPROX. 6 TO 7 QUARTS

If you like beets, you'll love Borscht! This fun spin on a Russian variety is a hearty meal even finicky eaters will enjoy. Serve hot or cold, and add a touch of sour cream and garnish with fresh sage. Feel free to add home canned sauerkraut to your borscht after heating a jar for serving.

24 medium beets, chopped

½ head red cabbage, sliced thin

2 cups Cabernet Sauvignon wine

3 Roma tomatoes, diced (1 cup)

2 medium onions, chopped (1 cup)

2 carrots, shredded (¾ cup)

12 garlic cloves, chopped

8 cups beef stock

1 tablespoon granulated sugar

1 tablespoon salt

1 teaspoon black pepper

1 Cut beet stems leaving 2 inches of stem and the root intact. Blanch beets for 30 minutes in boiling water then place beets in a bowl of cold water in the sink. Under a cold stream of water, use thumbs and slide beet skin off the beet. On a cutting board, remove stem and root, and discard. Chop beets and place in a stainless steel stockpot.

2 Add shredded red cabbage and wine to the beets. Over medium-high heat, bring mixture to a boil, then reduce heat and simmer for 10 minutes. Add tomatoes, onions, carrots, and garlic cloves and continue to boil for 5 minutes, stirring often. Remove from heat to cool.

3 Once cool enough to handle, work in batches to purée the mixture into a fine, smooth texture. Return puréed mixture to a clean stainless steel stockpot. Add the beef stock, sugar, salt, and black pepper and mix well. Bring to a quick boil on medium-high heat and boil for 5 minutes, stirring constantly to avoid scorching.

4 Using a funnel, ladle the borscht into jars leaving a 1-inch of headspace. Remove air bubbles and add additional borscht if necessary to maintain a 1-inch headspace.

5 Wipe the rim of each jar with a clean washcloth dipped in vinegar. Place a lid and ring on each jar and hand-tighten.

6 Place the jars in the pressure canner, lock the pressure canner lid, and bring the canner to a boil on high heat. Let the canner vent for 10 minutes. Process at 10 psi or according to your canner type and elevation. Process quarts for 90 minutes and pints for 75 minutes.

7 Allow canner to return to zero psi before removing the canner lid. Wait 5 minutes before removing the jars from the canner.

Chicken or Beef Fajitas

To the Jar

MAKES 5 QUARTS OR 10 PINTS

This delicious recipe has been all the rage, especially since canners have been using the raw stacking method more and more. Make this delicious meal in a jar using chicken, beef, or pork.

6 cups pinto beans

2 ½ cups sliced bell peppers, any color

2 ½ cups sliced sweet onions

5 Roma tomatoes, diced

5 chicken thighs, boneless skinless

5 small chicken breasts, boneless skinless

5 tablespoons fajita spice blend

8 cups chicken or beef broth

1 Using a funnel add the following to each quart jar: 1 cup beans, ½ cup peppers, ½ cup onions. If using pint jars, add half the amount to each pint. Press down ingredients to tightly pack.

2 Add one diced Roma tomato to each quart, or half a diced tomato to each pint. Slice one chicken thigh and one chicken breast into strips and add to each quart or use half if making pints. Add 1 heaping tablespoon of the fajita spice blend to each quart jar, or a heaping ½ tablespoon to each pint jar.

3 Next, slowly add chicken broth to ear jar, careful to leave a 1-inch headspace. Using the flip side of the headspace measuring tool, remove air bubbles by sliding the tool down the sides of the jar and pressing into the

jar's center mass. Add additional broth and repeat until there are no air pockets remaining and the broth is at 1-inch headspace.

4 Wipe the rim of each jar with a clean washcloth dipped in vinegar. Place a lid and ring on each jar and hand-tighten.

5 Place the jars in the pressure canner filled with 3 quarts of cool water, lock the pressure canner lid, and warm the canner on medium heat for 10 minutes. After canner has warmed, bring the canner to a boil on high heat. Let the canner vent for 10 minutes. Process at 10 psi or according to your canner type and elevation. Process quarts for 90 minutes and pints for 75 minutes.

6 Allow canner to return to zero psi before removing the canner lid. Wait 5 minutes before removing the jars from the canner.

Fajita Seasoning

Whisk together the following spices and store in a half-pint Mason jar:
6 tablespoons chili powder,
3 tablespoons ground cumin powder,
2 tablespoons brown sugar,
2 tablespoons paprika,
2 tablespoons garlic powder,
2 teaspoons ground mustard,
2 teaspoons salt,
1-3 teaspoons cayenne pepper,
1 teaspoon red pepper flakes,
and 1 teaspoon ground black pepper.

Irish Bean & Cabbage Stew

MAKES APPROX. 6 QUARTS OR 12 PINTS

This is my go-to lunch! Have fun substituting various vegetables and seasonings like white flesh potatoes for sweet potatoes, navy beans for pinto beans, red cabbage for green cabbage, or vegetable broth for beef broth.

Ingredients	Amount per Pint Jar	Amount per Quart Jar
3 cups dried pino beans	¼ cup	½ cup
3 cups diced onion	¼ cup	½ cup
4 celery stalks, chopped (2 cups)	1 tablespoon	2 tablespoons
12 garlic cloves, minced (3 tablespoons)	1 teaspoon	2 teaspoons
3 medium sweet potatoes, peeled and cubed (3 cups)	¼ cup	½ cup
9 carrots, peeled and chopped (3 cups)	¼ cup	½ cup
9 Roma tomatoes, diced (3 cups)	¼ cup	½ cup
½ head green cabbage, chopped (3 cups loosely packed)	¼ cup	½ cup
10 cups beef broth		

1 Using the list above, layer each of the ingredients in the order shown into jars.

2 After each ingredient is added, tap down. Be sure to maintain a 1-inch headspace when raw stacking. Press down on the final ingredient, chopped cabbage, to maintain the 1-inch headspace.

3 Slowly add the broth, one jar at a time, maintaining a 1-inch headspace. Use the air bubble remover tool to remove any trapped air bubbles. Lightly tap the jar on a cutting board to loosen any trapped air bubbles. Add additional broth to each jar to maintain the 1-inch of headspace.

4 Wipe the rim of each jar with a clean washcloth dipped in vinegar. Place a lid and ring on each jar and hand-tighten.

5 Place the jars in the pressure canner filled with 3 quarts of cool water, lock the pressure canner lid, and warm the canner on medium heat for 10 minutes. After canner has warmed, bring the canner to a boil on high heat. Let the canner vent for 10 minutes. Process at 10 psi or according to your canner type and elevation. Process quarts for 90 minutes and pints for 75 minutes.

6 Allow canner to return to zero psi before removing the canner lid. Wait 5 minutes before removing the jars from the canner.

Leila's Lamb

MAKES APPROX. 2 QUARTS OR 4 PINTS

To the Jar

This Middle Eastern dish boasts authentic flavors using ground lamb, pine nuts, and allspice. If you really want an authentic meal in a jar, swap out the paprika for sumac. While there are many ways to enjoy this dish, including heated in a saucepan and stuffing ½ cup into a pita with a couple tablespoons of tzatziki sauce and chopped Romain lettuce for the best lunch-on-the-go ever!

1 tablespoon extra-virgin olive oil

2 yellow onions, finely chopped (1 cup)

10 garlic cloves, minced (4 ½ tablespoons)

3 pounds ground lamb

3 Roma tomatoes, finely chopped (1 cup)

1 cup pine nuts

3 tablespoons ground allspice

1 tablespoon paprika

2 teaspoons salt

6 ounces tomato paste

1 In a deep skillet add olive oil, onions, and garlic. Over medium-high heat, cook until onions are translucent, about 8 minutes. Add the ground lamb, mix well and fully cook, about more 8 minutes. Add tomatoes, pine nuts, allspice, paprika, salt, and tomato paste. Stir and cook for an additional 5 minutes to blend all the spices and evenly disperse the tomato paste.

2 Using a funnel, ladle the mixture into jars leaving a 1-inch of headspace. Remove air bubbles and add additional mixture if necessary to maintain a 1-inch headspace.

3 Wipe the rim of each jar with a clean washcloth dipped in vinegar. Place a lid and ring on each jar and hand-tighten.

4 Place the jars in the pressure canner, lock the pressure canner lid, and bring the canner to a boil on high heat. Let the canner vent for 10 minutes. Process at 10 psi or according to your canner type and elevation. Process quarts for 90 minutes and pints for 75 minutes.

5 Allow canner to return to zero psi before removing the canner lid. Wait 5 minutes before removing the jars from the canner.

Ingredient Tip

If you do not have access to ground lamb, or do not eat it, feel free to substitute with ground beef and enjoy its splendor all the same.

Lamb & Spaghetti Squash Bake

MAKES APPROX. 2-4 SERVINGS

This simple fall meal is just another fun way to use Leila's Lamb. Simple, delicious, and packed with protein and fiber. If you do not have access to Spaghetti Squash, you may use Acorn or Butternut instead.

1 teaspoon brown sugar

½ teaspoon salt

1 medium spaghetti squash

1 tablespoon olive oil

2 teaspoons butter

1 pint jar Leila's Lamb

1 Preheat oven to 400°F.

2 Whisk together salt and sugar in a small bowl and divide in half. Cut spaghetti squash in half lengthwise.

Scoop out seeds and discard. Place each half-cut side up on a baking sheet. Drizzle olive oil over each and rub into squash to cover its flesh.

3 Sprinkle half the salt and sugar mixture over each piece of squash. Add 1 teaspoon of butter to each center of the squash. Place in oven and bake for 15 minutes.

4 Remove squash from oven and add half the pint jar of Leila's Lamb onto each piece of squash. Bake for an additional 10 minutes or until the squash is soft and can be pulled away from the skin.

5 Remove the cooked lamb and set aside. Using a fork, run it through the squash to produce spaghetti-like strands. Then, using a large spoon, scoop the squash out of the skin and plate alongside the lamb.

Recipe Tip

Wish to make a hearty lunch? Simply heat a pint jar of Leila's Lamb in a saucepan on the stovetop. Open two pita pockets and coat the interior generously with tzatziki sauce. Next, line each pita pocket with sliced red onions and chopped romaine lettuce. Add one cup of Leila's Lamb to each pita pocket and enjoy!

Glossary of Canning & Culinary Terms

Home Canning and preserving is very rewarding, but for those of you new to the science and math, canning can be quite daunting and often times challenging. Understanding the many terms used to describe various ingredients, techniques, and methodologies are the **building blocks** for a successful and safe canning experience. Confidently maneuver through any canning recipe or cookbook with this handy list of terms.

acetic acid: The component of vinegar that gives it a soured taste. The clear, liquid acid is the primary acid in vinegar. For pickling, vinegar must have 5 percent acetic acid.

acid: Most foods are somewhat acidic. Foods generally referred to as acidic include citrus juice, vinegar, and wine. Degree of acidity is measured on the pH scale; acids have a pH of less than 7. Acid ingredients react with bases to form salts and water. They have a sour taste. A chemical compound that yields hydrogen ions when in solution.

air bubble remover tool: The opposite end of a headspace measure tool used to release trapped air in jars packed with foods. It is also used to tamp down food in jars to pack more in. This tool can also be the handle of a wooden spoon, a small silicone spatula, or a chopstick.

aerobic bacteria: Bacteria that requires the presence of oxygen to function.

anaerobic environment: Means "without oxygen." An enclosed environment lacking free oxygen.

ascorbic acid: Another name for vitamin C. A water-soluble vitamin that is used in food preparation to minimize browning of some vegetables and fruits. Often used together with citric acid, which is derived from lemon or lime juice, in commercially prepared blends to treat fruits to prevent browning.

bacteria: Microorganisms found in the air, soil, and water. Harmful bacteria can survive in low-acid environments and produce toxins that can be deadly. For this reason, low-acid foods are pressure canned to enable heating to 240°F, a temperature that kills these bacteria.

blanch: The process of placing a food item in boiling water or steam for a short period of time followed by an ice water bath to quickly cool the food item and prevent further cooking. This process is used to inactivate enzymes in foods, as well as to loosen the skin or peel of some fruits and vegetables.

boil: Bringing a liquid to the temperature in which bubbles continuously break its surface. At sea level, the boiling point is 212°F, while at altitudes above 1,000 feet, this is achieved at a lower temperature.

boil, full rolling: Boiling that cannot be stirred down. This type of boiling, often accompanied by foaming, is essential when making cooked jams and jellies. The temperature to achieve a rolling boil is 220°F.

botulism: This is an uncommon, but potentially serious, type of food poisoning caused by ingesting the toxin produced by spores of the bacterium *Clostridium botulinum*. If vegetables and meats are not properly prepared and processed, any spore present in a sealed jar, which is an anaerobic environment, will survive and produce the toxin. Improperly processed low-acid foods are most susceptible. Using correct processing temperature and time to destroy the toxin-producing bacteria. Boiling foods for 10 minutes prior to consuming will kill the bacteria that produces the toxin.

brine: A solution used in the pickling process. Typically contains salt and water, although other ingredients such as spices or sugar can also be included.

butter (fat): A yellow to white solid emulsion of fat globules, water and sale produced by churning cows' milk. Butter has long been used as an edible cooking fat. It is comprised of 80% fat with almost no protein. Although may describe butter as a dairy product because it is derived from milk, butter contains nearly undetectable trace amounts of lactose making it safe for home canning. It is also high in acid with a pH of 6.1 to 6.4.

butter (fruit): A soft spread created using puréed fruit and sugar cooked over a low temperature until thickened. Best for tree and tropical fruits

canning liquid: Any liquid used in canning to cover food products in the jar. This can be water, brine, broth, syrup, or juice.

chutney: A sweet and sour condiment made from fruits or vegetables, vinegar, and spices. Best when cured for at least one month after canning to ensure flavors are well blended.

citric acid: An acid derived from citrus fruit. It is found in pectin and assists with gel formation, as well as commercial produce protectors to prevent oxidation of light-colored fruits.

citric acid bath: The blend of ½ cup bottled lemon juice with 8 cups water used to prevent fruit, and some vegetables, browning. Foods are submerged in the citric acid bath during preparation, then rinsed and used in canning and dehydrating recipes.

ClearJel® (Canning Gel): A thickening agent made from modified food starch that does not break down when heated to high temperatures or reheated after cooling. Commercially available and approved by the USDA for use in home canning.

conserve: Made from a combination of fruits, often including nuts, and frequently served with roasted meats.

dehydrate: To remove most of the moisture from food by drying it slowly in an oven or commercial dehydrator.

dial-gauge pressure canner: A pressure canner fitted with a one-piece 15 psi pressure regulator and a visual indicator (gauge) which provides the pounds of pressure within the canner.

dice: to cut into smaller pieces, roughly the size of ¼ inch or into small cubes no larger than ½ inch. To **finely dice,** cut food into $^1/_8$ inch size cubes.

dill: A pungent, aromatic herb that can be used fresh or dried. Fresh dill has feathery green leaves. The most useful dried form is dill seeds. In fresh preserving, dill is primarily used for pickling. One head of fresh dill is equivalent to 1 to 2 tsp (5 to 10 mL) dill seeds or 2 tsp (10 mL) dried dillweed.

dissolve: Stirring a dry substance into a liquid until solids are no longer remaining. For example, stirring salt into water to make pickling brine.

divided: Equally portioning dough before shaping or oil in batches for browning meat.

drain: to remove liquid from using a strainer or colander.

emulsion: A mixture of two or more liquids. There are three kinds of emulsions; temporary, semi-permanent and permanent. An example of a temporary emulsion is a simple vinaigrette which quickly separates after resting. Mayonnaise is an example of a permanent emulsion as there is no separation. Home canned emulsion soups such as Carrot Soup and Asparagus Soup are examples of semi-permanent emulsion as they will separate over time during long-term storage; however, with a quick shake of the jar or mix in the saucepan upon heating, the liquids will rejoin.

enzyme: A protein found in foods that begins the process of decomposition. Enzymes can change the texture, color, and flavor of fruits and vegetables. Food preservation methods deactivate these enzymes to permit long-term storage of foods.

exhausting (jar): Forcing air to escape from a closed jar by applying heat. As a food or liquid is heated, it expands upward and forces air from the jar through pressure buildup in the headspace.

first in, first out: An inventory rotation system to consume your older home canned goods before consuming those more recently preserved in a jar.

fold: To gently mix two or more ingredients together by softly lifting up and over from the sides to the center.

food poisoning: Any illness caused by the consumption of harmful bacteria and their toxins. The symptoms are usually gastrointestinal.

food mill: A mechanical kitchen tool used to purée soft foods. A food mill separates the skins and seeds of the fruits or vegetables on its top, and the puréed food is collected below.

fruit pectin: A substance found naturally in some fruits such as apples that possess the ability to gel liquids. It is an essential ingredient in making jelly and jam. Pectin can be purchased in powder and liquid form or created by finely dicing or mincing apples.

funnel: A plastic utensil that is placed in the mouth of a canning jar to allow for easy pouring of a food product into the jar. Funnels help prevent spillage and waste.

gasket: A rubber ring that sits along the inside circumference of a pressure canner lid and comes in contact with the base when locked into place. The gasket provides a seal between the lid and the base so steam cannot escape.

gelling agent: Any substance that acts to form a gel-like structure by binding liquid such as pectin or Canning Gel.

gel stage: The point at which a soft spread becomes a full gel. The gelling point is 220°F (104°C), or 8°F (4°C) above the boiling point of water.

gumbo: A Creole soup/stew thickened with file or okra.

hand-tighten: Also known as **fingertip-tight**, this is the degree to which a canning ring is turned by hand to properly secure it onto the screw bands of the glass canning jar. Turn the ring until resistance is met, then stop turning. Do not use the full force of your hands to overtighten the ring. If you feel you have overtightened the ring onto the screw bands, unscrew the ring, then turn back just until you feel the resistance stop.

hash: Chopped, cooked meat, usually with potatoes and/or other vegetables, which is seasoned, bound with a sauce, and sautéed. Also, to chop.

headspace: The space at the top of a canning jar that is left unfilled. Headspace varies based on the food type and is essential for creating a proper lid seal. Headspace measurements can range from ¼ inch to 1 ¼ inch, unless otherwise noted. A **generous inch headspace** would be 1 ¼ inch.

headspace measuring tool: This tool was created specifically for home canning to properly measure the free oxygen left in the interior of the jar after it is filled with food. It is notched to rest on the rim of the jar with etched measurements from ¼- to 1-inch.

hermetic seal: A seal so tight it prevents the passage of air or oxygen protecting home canned foods against the entry of microorganisms and maintains commercial sterility.

high-acid food: A food or recipe mixture with a pH value of 4.6 or lower. Fruits, fruit juices, tomatoes, jams, and jellies are naturally high-acid foods. Vinegar, citric acid, and lemon and lime juice lowers a recipe's pH, making the overall recipe a high-acid food. High-acid foods can be preserved safely by processing in a hot water bath using boiling water temperature of 212°F (100°C).

home canning: The process of preserving foods in glass jars by using time, temperature and acidity to properly kill harmful microorganisms and food-borne pathogens that cause spoilage and illness. The goal of home canning is to have a ready-made food source stored for long-term use and consumption.

hot-pack method: This method uses preheated, hot food to fill jars prior to processing. Filling jars with preheated food expels air from the fibers of the food and allows food to be packed more tightly.

infuse: Steeping an aromatic or other item in liquid to extract its flavor. Also, the liquid resulting from this process. In particular, this technique is used when making herb jelly or ginger tea.

ladle: A canning utensil with a long handle with a cup-shaped bowl at the end. It is used to carefully fill a Mason jar with a recipe. It is also used to serve soups, stews, and sauces.

legume: The mature seeds that grow inside pods, such as lentils, beans and peas. They are eaten for their earthy flavors and high nutritional value. Also, the French word for vegetable.

lemon juice: In home canning recipes, lemon juice is used to ensure the proper acidic pH level. Because the acid in fresh lemons is variable, it is important to use bottled lemon juice when the recipe specifies it to ensure the safety of the finished product. When fresh lemon juice is called for, either bottled or fresh can be used.

lentil: These are tiny bean-like seeds. They are one of the first plants used for foods. The Egyptians and Greeks cooked these small legumes and so did the Romans.

lid: A flat metal disc with a flanged edge lined with sealing compound used in combination with a metal screw band for vacuum-sealing fresh preserving jars. Reusable canning lids are often made of BPA plastic and the rubber sealing compound is a separate ring meant to be adhered to the plastic lid prior to affixing to the rim of the jar.

low-acid food: A food or recipe mixture with a pH value higher than 4.6. Vegetables, meat, poultry, and seafood are all low-acid foods. Low-acid foods rely solely on time and temperature to kill harmful microorganisms. Therefore, recipes with a 4.6 or higher pH value must be processed for longer and at a higher temperature from 240°F to 260°F (116°C to 127°C). Foods or recipes that are dense or a bit thicker will need additional time in the canner to ensure the heat fully penetrates each piece of food within the jar.

maple syrup: It is the first finished product made from boiled sap of the maple tree. Maple syrup may be used in canning recipes in place of sugar to sweeten the overall flavor.

microorganism: A living plant or animal of microscopic size, such as molds, yeasts or bacteria, that can cause spoilage in canned, refrigerated or frozen foods.

mince: Chop very fine.

mix: Combine ingredients, usually with a spoon or electric mixer, so they are all evenly blended.

mold: A superficial growth, often fuzzy in appearance, that produces especially on damp or decaying organic matter. Molds thrive on moisture and in a humid (warm) environment. Mold spores are everywhere and travel through the air. Highly acidic environments breaks down mold, vinegar kills about 82% of known molds. In home canning mold spores are easily destroyed when bringing recipes to temperatures between 140°F and 190°F (60°C and 88°C) or increasing the recipes acidic value. If mold forms in a jar of preserved food, it is likely due to an unsealed lid allowing free oxygen into the jar and the presence of moisture and humidity causing the food to decay.

oxidation of food: Also referred to as enzymatic browning, is the process of food turning brown due to the chemical reactions that takes place when foods are exposed to oxygen. The color darkens and the food begins to dry out. This may happen when certain fruits and vegetables are freshly cut. When home canning, this will (sometimes) happen if a jar siphoned liquid during processing and the food at the top of the jar is not covered by liquid. The food exposed to free oxygen in the jar will slightly darken and dry over time during long-term storage. So long as the lid remained sealed during storage, foods that have oxidized are safe to eat.

pectin: Pectin is a polysaccharide starch found in the cell walls of fruits and vegetables. In terms of food composition, pectin is a gelling agent derived solely from plants. It is available commercially in powder or liquid forms. Finely chopped apples are often used as natural pectin in canning recipes.

pH (potential of hydrogen): A measuring system in chemistry for determining the acidity or alkalinity of a solution, used in home canning to determine the processing method. In home canning, recipes are separated into high-acid and low-acid. Traditionally, a boiling water bather is used for processing high-acid foods and a pressure canner is used for processing both high- and low-acid foods.

pickle: The process of preserving food in a brine, which is a salt or vinegar solution.

pickling spice: A mixture of herbs and spices used to season pickles. Often includes dill weed and/or seed, coriander seed, cinnamon stick, peppercorns, bay leaves, and others.

pint: a unit of volume measurement equal to 16 fluid ounces. A common jar size when home canning because they can be double-stacked in a 23-quart pressure canner using a second flat rack.

preserves: A soft spread made with fruit and sugar. Preserves often have whole fruit pieces in them and can vary considerably in thickness, but typically do not hold their shape when spooned from the jar.

pressure canner: A tall pot with a locking lid, rack and a pressure-regulating mechanism that is used to process low-acid foods. The only kitchen appliance for canning that reaches 240°F (116°C) and higher, the temperature needed to kill harmful microorganisms.

pressure canning: This method of processing can be sued for both high- and low-acid foods, and many pressure canners double as a water bather simply by removing the rubber seal in the lid. Pressure canning relies on temperature of the pressurized air within the vessel, not on the water temperature. This way, a pressure canner can get upwards of 260°F (127°C), a temperature not achievable by boiling water. This is why pressure canning is recommended for processing low-acid foods. Prior to its invention, canners had to rely on extra time at 212°F (100°C) to preserve low-acid foods. [i.e. Canners would have to process meat for 3 hours in a water bath to ensure all microorganisms were killed. Today, because of the invention of a pressure canner, we can safely process meat in half the time.]

processing time: Time is one of the three main pillars behind the science and math in home canning. The other two pillars are pH value and temperature. The processing time is determined by the recipes' overall pH value, its density and the volume of food in each jar and temperature required during processing. Using these factors, the processing time is established. Time coupled with the acid, density and processing temperature will adequately kill any harmful microorganisms making foods safe for long-term storage.

purée: To process food by mashing, straining, or chopping it very finely to make it a smooth paste.

raw-pack: Tightly filling jars with raw, uncooked foods prior to heat processing.

reduce: A method of cooking liquids to evaporate water. This results in a liquid with a concentrated flavor. This liquid enhances broths and sauces in flavor and thickness. Also known as a reduction.

reconstitute: To restore dried, dehydrated or condensed food back to its original consistency and strength with the addition of liquid, usually water.

reprocessing: If you do not wish to refrigerate an unsealed jar and consume within a week, you may reprocess to make it shelf stable. Reprocessing is repeating the heat processing when a lid does not seal overnight, or within 8 to 12 hours. The original lid must be removed and the food and/or liquid brought to a boil, then simmered for 5 minutes. Repack the recipe into clean, hot jars, clean jar rims with vinegar, adhere new, clean lids, add screw bands and hand-tighten. The filled jars must then be reprocessed using the preserving method and processing time recommended in the recipe.

saucepan, large: An 8- to 10-quart (8 to 10 L) heavy pot essential for cooking jams, jellies, preserves and fruit butters. The pot must have a broad, flat bottom for good heat distribution and deep sides to prevent food from boiling over.

screw band: The glass threads at the top of each jar. The canning ring adheres to and tightens around these bands to keep the canning lid in place during processing.

sear: To brown food, usually meat, quickly over very high heat to seal in juices. This is usually the first step in a canning recipe using meat.

shelf stable: A home canned food or properly stored dried good that remains safe to eat without refrigeration for years.

shred: To cut, slice or tear food into thin strips. It is also referred to when pulling apart very tender cooked meats, like shredding a pork shoulder after smoking to create pulled pork.

simmer: Cooking food in a hot liquid that is heated to a boil then reduced, or is heated just below boiling point at temperatures 185°F to 210°F (85°C to 99°C). Small bubbles will rise to the surface of the liquid and collapse; the activity is much calmer than a full rolling boil.

slice: To cut foods across the grain into thin, uniform pieces.

spice bag: A small bag filled with herbs and spices that seeps flavor into food or liquid. Also referred to as a Sachet Bag in recipes.

Splenda®: This sugar substitute contains 95 percent dextrose and maltodextrin which the body readily metabolizes, combined with a small amount of mostly indigestible sucralose. It is 600 times sweeter than sugar in flavor. Splenda is higher in acid than regular sugar with a stable pH of 5 to 6. It can be used to replace sugar in canning recipes; however, it absorbs the liquid in each jar making the end product denser than when canning with sugar.

spoilage: The natural deterioration of food whereas when spoiled, it no longer is suitable to ingest. When home canning, we stop the natural decay of food by preserving its integrity by way of temperature, time and acid or a combination of the three in a hermetic environment without free oxygen. If food becomes spoiled in a jar during storage it is likely due to a lid failure or improper destruction of microorganisms. If your home canned good has spoiled you will notice one or more of the following: unsealed lid, mold, gassiness, cloudiness, see page outside of the jar, a pungent disagreeable odor, gradual discoloring of half of the food contents with the top half darker than the bottom half of the food contents, etc.

stevia: Stevia is a natural sweetener and sugar substitute derived from plant leaves of the Stevia rebaudiana plant from Brazil and Paraguay. The active compounds are steviol glycosides, which have 30 to 150 times the sweetness of sugar, are heat-stable and pH-stable, but are not fermentable. From a flavor perspective, Stevia is said to be 200 times sweeter than sugar. In plant form, stevia is alkaline with a 9.0 pH. When in a powder or liquid form, stevia has a pH is 5.8 making it lower in acid when canning. Stevia can be used in home canning to sweeten low-acid recipes or to add flavor to high-acid recipes; however, it is not advised to use Stevia to replace sugar when home canning fruit jams and spreads without testing the pH of the recipe to achieve 3.0 to 3.9 pH.

strain: To separate liquids from solids by passing through a sieve. Also, to sieve.

sugar: Sugar, or sucrose, is a carbohydrate occurring naturally in every fruit and vegetable in the plant kingdom. It is the product of photosynthesis when a plant transforms the sun's energy into food. Sugar used in cooking and baking is generally derived from sugar cane and sugar beets. Sugar is used as a sweetener and as a preservative for foods. Processed sugar has the addition of lime added to raise the pH to neutral pH of 7.0 or a pH as high as 9.0, making it lower in acid. Beet Sugar also have a neutral pH of 7.0 to 7.5. Brown sugar is higher in acid due to the moisture content of the molasses, ranging from 4.9 to 5.6 pH.

- *granulated sugar*: Fine or extra-fine white sugar crystals. Often referred to as "white sugar" in home baking and canning.

- *brown sugar*: Sugar crystals contained in a molasses syrup with natural flavor and color components. Dark and light brown sugars may be substituted according to individual preferences for product color or taste.

- *powdered sugar*: Also known as confectioners' sugar, is a very finely ground sugar made by milling sugar into a fine powdered state, used to make icing. This sugar is not used in home canning.

- *raw sugar*: About 98 percent sucrose and tan or brown in appearance; it is a coarse, granulated solid obtained on evaporation of clarified sugar cane juice.

- *turbinado sugar*: Raw sugar refined to a light tan color by washing in a centrifuge under sanitary conditions. Surface molasses is removed in the washing process and is closer to refined sugar than raw.

venting: The process used in pressure canning where the vent is left open while the water boils within the vessel permitting air to escape from the pressure canner. This stage in processing is accomplished prior to adhering the weighted gauge onto the vent pipe to build pressure in the vessel.

vessel: Another term used to describe the large pot, water bather or pressure canner which holds the water and jars when canning.

vinegar: A liquid solution of acetic acid and trace compounds from the substance of which it was derived. Typically contains 5 to 8 percent acetic acid produced by fermentation of ethanol or sugars by acetic acid bacteria. The Canning Diva® describes vinegar as being your "best friend" in the kitchen, especially when canning. Use 2 ounces in the vessel of your canner to keep your jars clean and free from mineral deposits when processing.

- *apple cider*: A vinegar produced from apples that has a tart, fruity flavor. Cider vinegar has a golden color and may discolor some canned foods. Always use 5 percent acidity when using cider vinegar for canning. May contain small amounts of malic acid and citric acid being it is derived from apples. Has a pH of 3.5 at a 5 percent strength.

- *malt*: Vinegar produced from the same grains used to make beer. It has a lemon, nutty and caramel flavor like malted ale. It is a more mild and sweeter flavor. Its pH is still acidic but less than white or cider vinegar and is often between 4 and 5 percent acidity. Safe for home canning and is often used to increase acid in a recipe or to enhance a recipe's flavor.

- white: A standard type of vinegar produced from grain alcohol with a sharp, pungent flavor. It is clear and colorless, making it suitable for a lot of different canning projects, as it does not compete with the colors or flavors of the foods. Always use 5 percent acidity vinegar when canning. Has a pH range of 2.5 to 2.7 and 2.4 at 5 percent strength.

- **wine, red or white**: Vinegar derived from wine, where the flavor reflects the source of the wine. Has a pH range of 2.6 to 2.8 making it high in acid but less than white vinegar. Safe for home canning and is often used to increase acid in a recipe or to enhance a recipe's flavor. Wine vinegar is typically 6 percent acidity or higher.

water-bath canner: A large pot and lid fixed with a rack to keep jars lifted away from the direct heat. The pot must be deep enough so jars are fully submerged and covered by 1-inch of water, as well as to allow the water to boil rapidly.

weighted-gauge pressure canner: A type of pressure canner that is fitted with either a three- or a one-piece weight. Weights typically measure in 5-, 10- and 15-lb to set specified pressure as indicated in the canning recipe. All weights are used when home canning; The 5-lb weight typically used when pressure canning fruits and other high-acid recipes, while 10- and 15-lb are used for low acid recipes. The weight used is dependent on the altitude in which you are canning. The weighted gauge will rock, or jiggle, causing it to make a ticking sound which is an audible indicator the pounds of pressure are accurate within the vessel.

Didn't find the term you're looking for? No worries!

Head over to my website at <u>canningdiva.com</u> to find an expanded list of canning and culinary terms.

Index

Index

About the Author

Diane Devereaux, The Canning Diva®, is a nationally syndicated food preservation expert, author, television presenter, instructor, and mother of two. Since 2012, Diane has been sharing her lifetime passion of canning and food preservation, translating it to the busy lives of families across the globe.

Diane started home canning in her thirteenth summer and was soon growing and maintaining her own garden. The experience quickly taught her the many benefits of natural pest control, crop rotation and healthy soil factors, heirloom seed production and collection, healthy meal creation, and of course, preserving her garden's beautiful bounty.

She received her bachelor's in international business from Davenport University and later plunged into a career in disaster management, where she applied her skills to those in crisis. Her background in home canning combined with her tenure in disaster management led Diane to create The Canning Diva®, where she blended her passion for gardening and preserving with her knowledge of preparedness and self-reliance. Today, she continues to educate others on home canning and food preservation with various culinary classes, an online Canning University, a weekly podcast *Canning with The Diva!*™, and numerous YouTube videos.

Follow The Canning Diva®

www.canningdiva.com